AN APPEAL TO ALL THOSE
TRUTHS OF TH_
BY
William Law

AN APPEAL TO ALL THOSE THAT DOUBT THE TRUTHS OF THE GOSPEL

Published by Scriptura Press

New York City, NY

First published 1893

Copyright © Scriptura Press, 2015

All rights reserved

Except in the United States of America, this book is sold subject to the condition that it shall not, by way of trade or otherwise, be lent, re-sold, hired out, or otherwise circulated without the publisher's prior consent in any form of binding or cover other than that in which it is published and without a similar condition including this condition being imposed on the subsequent purchaser.

ABOUT SCRIPTURA PRESS

Scriptura Press is a Christian company that makes Christian works available and affordable to all. We are a non-denominational publishing group that shares the teachings of the Scripture, whether in the form of sermons or histories of the Church.

An Appeal to All Those that Doubt the Truths of the Gospel

WHETER

They DEISTS, ARIANS, SOCINIANS, or Nominal christians.

In which, the true Grounds and Reasons of the whole Christian Faith and Life are plainly and fully demonstrated.

Chapter I

A Of Creation in general. **B** Of the Origin of the Soul. **C** Whence Will and Thought are in the Creature. **D** Why the Will is free. **E** The Origin of Evil solely from the Creature. **F** This World not a first, immediate Creation of God. **G** How the World comes to be in its present State. **H** The first Perfection of Man. **I** All Things prove a Trinity in God. **J** Man hath the triune Nature of God in Him. **K** Arianism and Deism confuted by Nature. **L** That Life is uniform through all Creatures. **M** That there is but one kind of Death to be found in all Nature. **N** The fallen Soul hath the Nature of Hell in it. **O** Regeneration is a real Birth of a Divine Life in the Soul. **P** That there is but one Salvation possible in Nature. **Q** This Salvation only to be had from Jesus Christ. **R** All the Deist's Faith and Hope proved to be false.

A/B [App-1-1] It has been an opinion commonly received, though without any foundation in the light of nature, or scripture, that God created this whole visible world, and all things in it, out of nothing. Nay, that the souls of men, and the highest orders of beings, were created in the same manner. The scripture is very decisive against this original of the souls of men. For Moses saith, "God breathed into man (Spiraculum Vitarum) the breath of lives, and man became a living soul." Here the notion of a soul created out of nothing, is in the plainest, strongest manner rejected, by the first written Word of God; and no Jew or Christian can have the least excuse for falling into such an error; here the highest and most divine original is not darkly, but openly, absolutely, and in the strongest form of expression ascribed to the soul; it came forth as a breath of life, or lives, out from the mouth of God, and therefore did not come out of the womb of nothing, but is what it is, and has what it has in itself, from, and out of the first and highest of all beings.

[App-1-2] For to say that God breathed forth into man the breath of lives, by which he became a living soul, is directly saying, that that which was life, light, and Spirit in the living God, was breathed forth from him to become the life, light and spirit of a creature. The soul therefore being declared to be an effluence from God, a breath of God, must have the nature and likeness of God in it, and is, and can be nothing else, but something, or so much of the divine nature, become creaturely existing, or breathed forth from God, to stand before him in the form of a creature.

[App-1-3] When the animals of this world were to be created, it was only said, Let the earth, the air, the water bring forth creatures after their kinds; but when man was to be brought forth, it was said, "Let us make man in our own image and likeness." Is not this directly saying, Let man have his beginning and being out of us, that he may be so related to us in his soul and spirit, as the animals of this world are related to the elements from which they are produced. Let him so come forth from us, be so breathed out of us, that our triune, divine nature may be manifested in him, that he may stand before us as a creaturely image, likeness, and representative of that which we are in ourselves.

[App-1-4] Now, from this original doctrine of the creation of man, known to all the first inhabitants of the world, and published in the front of the first written Word of God; these great truths have been more or less declared to all the nations of the world. First, that all mankind are the created offspring of the one God. Secondly, that in all men there is a spirit or breath of lives, that did not begin to be out of nothing, or was created out of nothing; but came from the true God into man, as his own breath of life breathed into him. Thirdly, that therefore there is in all men, wherever dispersed over the earth, a divine, immortal, never-ending spirit, that can have nothing of death in it, but must live for ever, because it is the breath of the everliving God. Fourthly, that by this immortal breath, or Spirit of God in man, all mankind stand in the same nearness of relation to God, are all equally his children, are all under the same necessity of paying the same homage of love and obedience to him, all fitted to receive the same blessing and happiness from him, all created for the same eternal enjoyment of his love and presence with them, all equally called to worship and adore him in spirit and truth, all equally capable of seeking and finding him, of having a blessed union and communion with him.

[App-1-5] These great truths, the first pillars of all true and spiritual religion, on which the holy and divine lives of the ancient patriarchs was supported, by which they worshipped God in a true and right faith; these truths, I say, were most eminently and plainly declared in the express letter of the Mosaic writings, here quoted. And no writer, whether Jewish or Christian, has so plainly, so fully, so deeply laid open the true ground, and necessity of an eternal, never- ceasing relation between God, and all the human nature; no one has so incontestably asserted the immortality of the soul, or spirit of man; or so deeply laid open, and proved the necessity of one religion, common to all human nature, as the legislator of the Jewish theocracy had done. Life and immortality are indeed justly said to be brought to light by the gospel; not only because they there stand in a new degree of light, largely explained, and much appealed to, and absolutely promised by the Son of God himself, but chiefly because the precious means and mysteries of obtaining a blessed life, and a blessed immortality, were only revealed, or brought to light by the gospel.

[App-1-6] But the incontestable ground and reason of an immortal life, and eternal relation between God, and the whole human nature, and which lays all mankind under the same obligations to the same true worship of God, is most fully set forth by Moses, who alone tells us the true fact; how, and why man is immortal in his nature, viz., because the beginning of his life was a breath, breathed into him from God; and for this end, that he might be a living image and likeness of God, created to partake of the nature and immortality of God.

[App-1-7] This is the great doctrine of the Jewish legislator, and which justly places him amongst the greatest preachers of true religion. St. Paul used a very powerful argument to persuade the Athenians to own the true God, and the true religion, when he told them, "that God made the world and all things therein; that he giveth life and breath and all things; that he hath made of one blood, all nations of men to dwell on the earth; that they should all seek the Lord, if haply they might feel after, and find him, seeing he is not far from any of us, because in him we live, move, and have our being." {Acts xvii.24.} And yet this doctrine, which St. Paul preaches to the Athenians, is nothing else, but that same divine and heavenly instruction, which he had learnt from Moses, which Moses openly and plainly taught all the Jews. The Jewish theocracy therefore was by no means an intimation to that people, that they had no concern with the true

God, but as children of this world, under his temporal protection or punishment; for their lawgiver left them no room for such a thought, because he had as plainly taught them their eternal nature and eternal relation, which they had to God in common with all mankind; as St. Paul did to the Athenians, who only set before them that very doctrine that Moses taught all the Jews. The great end of the Jewish theocracy was to show, both to Jew and gentile, the absolute, uncontrollable power of the one God, by such a covenanted interposition of his providence, that all the world might know, that the one God, from whom both Jew and gentile were fallen away, by departing from the faith and religion of their first fathers, was the only God, from whom all mankind could receive either blessing or cursing.

[App-1-8] This was the great thing intended to be proclaimed to all the world by this theocracy, viz., that only the God of Israel had power to save or destroy, to punish or reward, according to his pleasure; and that therefore all the gods of the heathens, were mere vanity. If therefore any Jews, by reason of those extraordinary temporal blessings and cursings which they received under their theocracy, grew grossly ignorant, or dully senseless of their eternal nature, and eternal relation to God, and of that one true religion, which by nature they were obliged to observe in common with all mankind; if they took God only to be their local or tutelary deity, and themselves to be only animals of this world; such a grossness of belief was no more to be charged upon their great lawgiver, Moses, than if they had believed, that a golden calf was their true god. But to return to the creation.

B   [App-1-9] 2. It is the same impossibility for a thing to be created out of nothing, as to be created by nothing. {See Spirit of Prayer, Part II, page 58, &c. Way to Divine Knowledge, page 247, &c.} It is no more a part, or prerogative of God's omnipotence to create a being out of nothing, than to make a thing to be, without any one quality of being in it; or to make, that there should be three, where there is neither two, nor one. Every creature is nothing else, but nature put into a certain form of existence; and therefore a creature not formed out of nature, is a contradiction. A circle, or a square cannot be made out of nothing, nor could any power bring them into existence, but because there is an extension in nature, that can be put into the form of a circle, or a square: but if dead figures cannot by any power be made out of nothing, who sees not the impossibility of making living creatures, angels, and the souls of men out of nothing?

C   [App-1-10] 3. Thinking and willing are eternal, they never began to be. Nothing can think, or will now, in which there was not will and thought from all eternity. For it is as possible for thought in general to begin to be, as for that which thinks in a particular creature to begin to be of a thinking nature: therefore the soul, which is a thinking, willing being is come forth, or created out of that which hath willed and thought in God, from all eternity. The created soul is a creature of time, and had its beginning on the sixth day of the creation; but the essences of the soul, which were then formed into a creature, and into a state of distinction from God, had been in God from all eternity, or they could not have been breathed forth from God into the form of a living creature.

[App-1-11] And herein lies the true ground and depth of the uncontrollable freedom of our will and thoughts: they must have a self- motion, and self-direction, because they came out of the self-existent God. They are eternal, divine powers, that never began to be, and therefore cannot begin to be in subjection to any thing. That which thinks and wills in the soul, is that very same unbeginning breath which thought and willed in God, before it was breathed into the form of an human soul; and therefore it is, that will and thought cannot be bounded or constrained.

[App-1-12] Herein also appears the high dignity, and never-ceasing perpetuity of our nature. The essences of our souls can never cease to be, because they never began to be: and nothing can live eternally, but that which hath lived from all eternity. The essences of our soul were a breath in God before they became a living soul, they lived in God before they lived in the created soul, and therefore the soul is a partaker of the eternity of God, and can never cease to be. Here, O man, behold the great original, and the high state of thy birth; here let all that is within thee praise thy God, who has brought thee into so high a state of being, who has given thee powers as eternal and boundless as his own attributes, that there might be no end or limits of thy happiness in him. Thou begannest as time began, but as time was in eternity before it became days and years, so thou wast in God before thou wast brought into the creation: and as time is neither a part of eternity, nor broken off from it, yet come out of it; so thou art not a part of God, nor broken off from him, yet born out of him. Thou shouldst only will that which God willeth, only love that which he loveth, cooperate, and unite with him in the whole form of thy life; because all that thou art, all that thou hast, is only a spark of his own life and Spirit derived into thee. If thou desirest, and turn towards the sun, all the blessings of the Deity will spring up in thee; Father, Son, and Holy Ghost, will make their abode with thee. If thou turnest in towards thyself, to live to thyself, to be happy in the workings of an own will, to be rich in the sharpness and acuteness of thy own reason, thou choosest to be a weed, and canst only have such a life, spirit and blessing from God, as a thistle has from the sun. But to return.

[App-1-13] 4. To suppose a willing, understanding being, created out of nothing, is a great absurdity. For as thinking and willing must have always been from all eternity, or they could never have been either in eternity, or time; so, wherever they are found in any particular, finite beings, they must of all necessity, be direct communications, or propagations of that thinking and willing, which never could begin to be.

[App-1-14] The creation therefore of a soul, is not the creation of thinking and willing, or the making that to be, and to think, which before had nothing of being, or thought; but it is the bringing the powers of thinking and willing out of their eternal state in the one God, into a beginning state of a self-conscious life, distinct from God. And this is God's omnipotent, creating ability, that he can make the powers of his own nature become creatural, living, personal images of what he is in himself, in a state of distinct personality from him: so that the creature is one, in its finite, limited state, as God is one, and yet hath nothing in it, but that which was in God before it came into it: for the creature, be it what it will, high or low, can be nothing else, but a limited participation of the nature of the creator. Nothing can be in the creature, but what came from the creator, and the creator can give nothing to the creature, but that which it hath in itself to give. And if beings could be created out of nothing, the whole creation could be no more a proof of the being of God, than if it had sprung up of itself out of nothing: for if they are brought into being out of nothing, then they can have nothing of God in them; and so can bear no testimony of God; but are as good a proof, that there is no God, as that there is one. But if they have anything of God in them, then they cannot be said to be created out of nothing.

[App-1-15] 5. That the souls of men were not created out of nothing, but are born out of an eternal original, is plain from hence; from that delight in, and desire of eternal existence, which is so strong and natural to the soul of man. For nothing can delight in, or desire eternity, or so much as form a notion of it, or think upon it, or any way reach after it, but that alone which is generated from it, and come out of it. For it is a self-evident truth, that nothing can look higher, or further back, than into its own original; and therefore, nothing can look or reach back into eternity, but that which came out of it. This is as certain, as that a line reaches, and can reach no further back, than to that point from whence it arose.

[App-1-16] Our bodily eyes are born out of the firmamental light of this world, and therefore they can look no further than the firmament: but our thoughts know no bounds; therefore they are come out of that which is boundless. The eyes of our minds can look as easily backwards into that eternity which always hath been, as into that which ever shall be; and therefore it is plain, that that which thinks and wills in us, which so easily, so delightfully, so naturally penetrates into all eternity, has always had an eternal existence, and is only a ray or spark of the divine nature, brought out into the form of a creature, or a limited, personal existence, by the creating power of God.

[App-1-17] 6. Again. Every soul shrinks back, and is frightened at the very thought of falling into nothing. Now this undeniably proves, that the soul was not created out of nothing. For it is an eternal truth, spoken by all nature, that everything strongly aspires after, and cannot be easy, till it finds and enjoys that original out of which it arose. If the soul therefore was brought forth out of nothing, all its being would be a burden to it; it would want to be dissolved, and to be delivered from every kind and degree of sensibility; and nothing could be so sweet and agreeable to it, as to think of falling back into that nothingness, out of which it was called forth by its creation. Thus is the eternal, immortal, divine nature of the soul, which the schools prove with so much difficulty one of the most obvious, self-evident truths in all nature. For nothing but that which is eternal in its own nature, can have the least thought about eternity.

[App-1-18] If a beast had not the nature of the earth in it, nothing that is on the earth, or springs out of it, could be in the least degree agreeable to it, or desired by it. If the soul had not the nature of eternity in it, nothing that is eternal could give it the smallest pleasure, or be able to make any kind of impression upon it. For as nothing can taste, or relish, or enter into the agreeable sensations of this world, but that which hath the nature of this world in it; so nothing can taste, or relish, or look into eternity with any kind of pleasure, but that which hath the nature of eternity in it.

[App-1-19] 7. If the soul was not born, or created out of God, it could have no happiness in God, no desire, nor any possibility of enjoying him. If it had nothing of God in it, it must stand in the utmost distance of contrariety to him, and be utterly incapable of living, moving, and having its being in God: for everything must have the nature of that, out of which it was created, and must live, and have its being in that root or ground from whence it sprung. If therefore there was nothing of God in the soul, nothing that is in God could do the soul any good, or have any kind of communication with it; but the gulf of separation between God and the soul, would be even greater than that which is between heaven and hell.

[App-1-20] 8. But let us rejoice, that our soul is a thinking, willing being, full of thoughts, cares, longings, and desires of eternity; for this is our full proof, that our descent is from God himself, that we are born out of him, breathed forth from him; that our soul is of an eternal nature, made a thinking, willing, understanding creature out of that which hath willed and thought in God from all eternity; and therefore must, for ever and ever, be a partaker of the eternity of God.

[App-1-21] And here you may behold the sure ground of the absolute impossibility of the annihilation of the soul. Its essences never began to be, and therefore can never cease to be; they had an eternal reality before they were in, or became a distinct soul, and therefore they must have the same eternal reality in it. It was the eternal breath of God before it came into man, and therefore the eternity of God must be inseparable from it. It is no more a property of the divine omnipotence to be able to annihilate a soul, than to be able to make an eternal truth become a fiction of yesterday: and to think it a lessening of the power of God, to say, that he cannot annihilate the soul, is as absurd, as to say, that it is a lessening of the light of the sun, if it cannot destroy, or darken its own rays of light.

[App-1-22] O, dear reader, stay a while in this important place, and learn to know thyself: all thy senses make thee to know and feel, that thou standest in the vanity of time; but every motion, stirring, imagination, and thought of thy mind, whether in fancying, fearing, or loving everlasting life, is the same infallible proof, that thou standest in the midst of eternity, art an offspring and inhabitant of it, and must be for ever inseparable from it. Ask when the first thought sprung up, find out the birth-day of truth, and then thou wilt have found out, when the essences of thy soul first began to be. Were not the essences of thy soul as old, as unbeginning, as unchangeable, as everlasting as truth itself, truth would be at the same distance from thee, as absolutely unfit for thee, as utterly unable to have any communion with thee, as to be the food of a worm.

[App-1-23] The ox could not feed upon the grass, or receive any delight or nourishment from it, unless grass and the ox had one and the same earthly nature and original; thy mind could receive no truth, feel no delight and satisfaction in the certainty, beauty, and harmony of it, unless truth and the mind stood both in the same place, had one and the same unchangeable nature, unbeginning original. If there will come a time, when thought itself shall cease, when all the relations and connections of truth shall be untied; then, but not till then, shall the knot, or band of thy soul's life be unloosed. It is a spark of the Deity, and therefore has the unbeginning, unending life of God in it. It knows nothing of youth, or age, because it is born eternal. It is a life that must burn for ever, either as a flame of light and love in the glory of the divine majesty, or as a miserable firebrand in that god, which is a consuming fire.

[App-1-24] 9. It is impossible, that this world, in the state and condition it is now in, should have been an immediate and original creation of God: this is as impossible, as that God should create evil, either natural or moral. That this world hath evil in all its parts; that its matter is in a corrupt, disordered state, full of grossness, disease, impurity, wrath, death and darkness, is as evident, as that there is light, beauty, order and harmony everywhere to be found in it. Therefore it is as impossible, that this outward state and condition of things, should be a first and immediate work of God, as that there should be good and evil in God himself. All storms and tempests, every fierceness of heat, every wrath of cold proves with the same certainty, that outward nature is not a first work of God, as the selfishness, envy, pride, wrath, and malice of devils, and men proves, that they are not in the first state of their creation. As no kind or degree of moral evil could possibly have its cause in, or from God, so there cannot be the least shadow of imperfection and disorder in outward nature, but what must have sprung up in the same manner, and from the same causes, as sickness and corrupt flesh is come into the human body, namely, from the sin of the creature. Storms, tempests, gravel, stone, sour and dead earth are the same things, the same diseases, the same effects of sin, produced in the same manner in the outward body of nature, as corrupt flesh, fevers, dropsies, plagues, gravel, stone, and gout, are produced in the outward body of man. For that, and that only which produces stone in the body of man, did produce stone in the outward nature, as shall plainly appear by and by. For nature within, and without man, is one and the same, and has but one and the same way of working; a stone in the body, and a stone out of the body of man, proceeds from one and the same disorder of nature.

[App-1-25] When therefore you see a diseased, gouty, leprous, asthmatical, scorbutic man, you can with the utmost certainty say, this is not that human body which God first created in paradise; so, when you see the disorders of heat and cold, the poisonous earth, unfruitful seasons, and malignant qualities of outward nature, you can with the same certainty affirm, this state of nature is not a first creation of God, but that same must have happened to it, which has happened to the body of man. For dark, sour, hard, dead earth, can no more be a first, immediate creation of God, than a wrathful devil, as such, can be created by him. For dark, sour, dead earth is as disordered in its kind, as the devils are, and has as certainly lost its first heavenly condition and nature, as the devils have lost theirs. But now, as in man, the little world, there is excellency and perfection enough to prove, that human nature is the work of an all-perfect being, yet, so much impurity and disease of corrupt flesh and blood, as undeniably shows, that sin has almost quite spoiled the work of God. So, in the great world, the footsteps of an infinite wisdom in the order and harmony of the whole, sufficiently appears; yet, the disorders, tumults, and evils of nature, plainly demonstrate, that the present condition of this world is only the remains or ruins, first, of a heaven spoiled by the fall of angels, and then of a paradise lost by the sin of man. So that man, and the world in which he lives, lie both in the same state of disorder and impurity, have both the same marks of life and death in them, both bring forth the same sort of evils, both want a redeemer, and have need of the same kind of death and resurrection, before they can come to their first state of purity and perfection.

[App-1-26] 10. That this outward world was not created out of nothing, is plainly taught by St. Paul, who declares, Rom.i.20, that the creation of the world is out of the invisible things of God;

so that the outward condition and frame of invisible nature, is a plain manifestation of that spiritual world from whence it is descended. For as every outside necessarily supposes an inside, and as temporal light and darkness must be the product of eternal light and darkness, so this outward, visible state of things necessarily supposes some inward, invisible state, from whence it is come into this degree of outwardness. Thus all that is on earth is only a change or alteration of something that was in heaven: and heaven itself is nothing else but the first glorious out-birth, the majestic manifestation, the beatific visibility of the one God in Trinity. And thus we find out, how this temporal nature is related to God; it is only a gross out-birth of that which is an eternal nature, or a blessed heaven, and stands only in such a degree of distance from it, as water does to air; and this is the reason why the last fire will, and must turn this gross, temporal nature into its first, heavenly state. But to suppose the gross matter of this world to be made out of nothing, or compacted nothing, is more absurd, than to suppose ice that has congealed nothing, a yard that is not made up of inches, or a pound that is not the product of ounces.

[App-1-27] 11. And indeed to suppose this, or any other material world to be made out of nothing, has all the same absurdities in it, as the supposing angels and spirits, to be created out of nothing.

[App-1-28] All the qualities of all beings are eternal; no real quality or power can appear in any creature, but what has its eternal root, or generating cause in the creator. If a quality could begin to be in a creature, which did not always exist in the creator, it would be no absurdity to say, that a thing might begin to be, without any cause either of its beginning, or being. All qualities, properties, or whatever can be affirmed of God, are self-existent, and necessary existent. Self and necessary existence is not a particular attribute of God, but is the general nature of everything that can be affirmed of God. All qualities and properties are self-existent in God: now, they cannot change their nature when they are derived, or formed into creatures, but must have the same self-birth, and necessary existence in the creature, which they had in the creator. The creature begins to be, when, and as it pleased God; but the qualities which are become creaturely, and which constitute the creature, are self-existent, just as the same qualities are in God. Thus, thinking, willing, and desire can have no outward maker, their maker is in themselves, they are self- existent powers wherever they are, whether in God, or in the creature, and as they form themselves in God, so they form themselves in the creature. But now, if no quality can begin to be, if all the qualities and powers of creatures must be eternal and necessary existent in God, before they can have any existence in any creature; then it undeniably follows, that every created thing must have its whole nature from, and out of the divine nature.

[App-1-29] All qualities are not only good, but infinitely perfect, as they are in God; and it is absolutely impossible, that they should have any evil or defect in them, as they are in the one God, who is the great and universal all. Because, where all properties are, there must necessarily be an all possible perfection: and that which must always have all in itself, must, by an absolute necessity, be always all perfect. But the same qualities, thus infinitely good and perfect in God, may become imperfect and evil in the creature; because in the creature, being limited and finite, they may be divided and separated from one another by the creature itself. Thus strength and fire in the divine nature, are nothing else but the strength and flame of love, and never can be anything else; but in the creature, strength and fire may be separated from love, and then they are become an evil, they are wrath and darkness, and all mischief: and thus that same strength and quality, which in creatures making a right use of their own will, or self-motion, becomes their goodness and perfection, doth in creatures making a wrong use of their will, become their evil and mischievous nature; and it is a truth that deserves well to be considered, that there is no goodness in any creature, from the highest to the lowest, but in its continuing to be such an union of qualities and powers, as God has brought together in its creation.

[App-1-30] In the highest order of created beings, this is their standing in their first perfection, this is their fulfilling of the whole will or law of God, this is their piety, their song of praise, their eternal adoration of their great creator. On the other hand, there is no evil, no guilt, no deformity in any creature, but in its dividing and separating itself from something which God had given to be in union with it. This, and this alone, is the whole nature of all good, and all evil in the creature, both in the moral and natural world, in spiritual and material things. For instance, dark, fiery wrath in the soul, is not only very like, but it is the self-same thing in the soul which a wrathful poison is in the flesh. Now, the qualities of poison are in themselves, all of them good qualities, and necessary to every life; but they are become a poisonous evil, because they are separated from some other qualities. Thus also the qualities of fire and strength that constitute an evil wrath in the soul, are in themselves very good qualities, and necessary to every good life; but they are become an evil wrath, because separated from some other qualities with which they should be united.

[App-1-31] The qualities of the devil and all fallen angels, are good qualities; they are the very same which they received from their infinitely perfect creator, the very same which are, and must be in all heavenly angels; but they are an hellish, abominable malignity in them now, because they have, by their own self-motion, separated them from the light and love which should have kept them glorious angels.

[App-1-32] And here may be seen at once, in the clearest light, the true origin of all evil in the creation, without the least imputation upon the creator. God could not possibly create a creature to be an infinite all, like himself: God could not bring any creature into existence, but by deriving into it the self-existent, self-generating, self-moving qualities of his own nature: for the qualities must be in the creature, that which they were in the creator, only in a state of limitation; and therefore, every creature must be finite, and must have a self-motion, and so must be capable of moving right and wrong, of uniting or dividing from what it will, or of falling from that state in which it ought to stand: but as every quality, in every creature, both within and without itself is equally good, and equally necessary to the perfection of the creature, since there is nothing that is evil in it, nor can become evil to the creature, but from itself, by its separating that from itself, with which it can, and ought to be united, it plainly follows, that evil can no more be charged upon God, than darkness can be charged upon the sun; because every quality is equally good, every quality of fire is as good as every quality of light, and only becomes an evil to that creature, who, by his own self-motion, has separated fire from the light in his own nature.

[App-1-33] 12. If a delicious, fragrant fruit had a power of separating itself from that rich spirit, fine taste, smell, and color which it receives from the virtue of the sun, and the spirit of the air; or if it could in the beginning of its growth, turn away from the sun, and receive no virtue from it, then it would stand in its own first birth of wrath, sourness, bitterness, and astringency, just as the devils do, who have turned back into their own dark root, and rejected the Light and Spirit of God: so that the hellish nature of a devil is nothing else, but its own first forms of life, withdrawn, or separated from the heavenly light and love; just as the sourness, astringency, and bitterness of a fruit, are nothing else but the first forms of its own vegetable life before it has reached the virtue of the sun, and the spirit of the air.

[App-1-34] And as a fruit, if it had a sensibility of itself, would be full of torment, as soon as it was shut up in the first forms of its life, in its own astringency, sourness, and stinging bitterness: so the angels, when they had turned back into these very same first forms of their own life, and broken off from the heavenly light and love of God, they became their own hell. No hell was made for them, no new qualities came into them, no vengeance or pains from the God of love fell upon them; they only stood in that state of division and separation from the Son, and Holy Spirit of God, which, by their own motion, they had made for themselves. They had nothing in them, but what they had from God, the first forms of an heavenly life, nothing but what the most heavenly beings have, and must have, to all eternity; but they had them in a state of self-torment, because they had separated them from that birth of light and love, which alone could make them glorious sons, and blessed images of the Holy Trinity.

[App-1-35] The same strong desire, fiery wrath, and stinging motion is in holy angels, that is in devils, just as the same sourness, astringency, and biting bitterness is in a full ripened fruit, which was there before it received the riches of the light and spirit of the air. In a ripened fruit, its first sourness, astringency, and bitterness is not lost, nor destroyed, but becomes the real cause of all its rich spirit, fine taste, fragrant smell, and beautiful color; take away the working, contending nature of these first qualities, and you annihilate the spirit, taste, smell, and virtue of the fruit, and there would be nothing left for the sun and the spirit of the air to enrich.

[App-1-36] Just in the same manner, that which in a devil is an evil selfishness, a wrathful fire, a stinging motion, is in an holy angel, the everlasting kindling of a divine life, the strong birth of an heavenly love, it is a real cause of an everlasting, ever-triumphing joyfulness, an ever-increasing sensibility of bliss.

[App-1-37] Take away the working, contending nature of these first qualities, which in a devil, are only a serpentine selfishness, wrath, fire, and stinging motion; take away these, I say, from holy angels, and you leave them neither light, nor love, nor heavenly glory, nothing for the birth of the Son, Holy Spirit of God to rise up in.

[App-1-38] So that here you may see this glorious truth, that the love and goodness of God is as plain and undeniable in having given to the fallen angels, those very qualities and powers which are now their hell, as in giving the first sourness, astringency and bitterness to fruits, which alone makes them capable of their delicious spirit, taste, color, and smell.

[App-1-39] 13. And thus you see the uniform life of all the creatures of God; how they are all raised, enriched, and blessed by the same life of God, derived into different kingdoms of creatures. For the beginnings and progress of a perfect life in fruits, and the beginnings and progress of a perfect life in angels, are not only like to one another, but are the very same thing, or the workings of the very same qualities, only in different kingdoms. Astringency in a fruit, is the very same quality, and does the same work in a fruit, that attracting desire does in a spiritual being; it is the same beginner, former, and supporter of a creaturely life in the one, as in the other. No creature in heaven, or earth, can begin to be, but by this astringency, or desire, being made the ground of it: and yet this astringency kept from the virtue of the sun, can only produce a poisonous fruit, and this astringent desire in an angel, turned from the light of God, can only make a devil. The biting, stinging bitterness of a fruit, if you could add thought to it, would be the very gnawing envy of the devil: and the envious motion in the devil's nature, would be nothing else but that stinging bitterness which is in a fruit, if you could take thought from the devil's motion.

[App-1-40] 14. From this attraction, astringency, or desire, which is one and the same quality in every individual thing, which is the first form of being and life, the very ground of every creature, from the highest angel to the lowest vegetable, we are led by an unerring thread to the first desire, or that desire which is in the divine nature. For as this attraction, or astringent desire is in spiritual and corporeal things, one and the same quality, working in the same manner, so is it one and the same quality with that first, unbeginning desire, which is in the divine nature.

[App-1-41] That there is an attracting desire in the divine nature, is undeniable, because attraction is essential to all bodies; and desire, which is the same quality, is absolutely inseparable from all intelligible beings; therefore, that which is necessarily existent in the creature, upon the supposition of its creation, must necessarily be in the creator; because no inherent, operative quality can be in the creature, unless the same kind of quality had always been in the creator: therefore, attraction or desire, which are inseparable from every created being and life, are only various participations of the divine nature; or emanations from it, formed into different kingdoms of creatures, and working in all of them according to their respective natures.

[App-1-42] In vegetables, it is that attraction, or desire, which brings every growing thing to its highest perfection: in angels, it is that blessed hunger, by which they are filled with the divine nature: in devils, it is turned into that serpentine selfishness, or crooked desire, which makes them a hell and torment to themselves.

[App-1-43] 15. On the other hand, as we thus prove a posteriori, from a view of the creature, that there must be an attracting desire in the divine nature; so we can prove a priori also, from a consideration of God, that there must be an attracting desire in everything that ever was, or can be created by God: for nothing can come into being, but because God wills and desires it; therefore the desire of God is the creator, the original of everything. The creating will, or desire of God, is not a distant, or separate thing, as when a man wills or desires something to be done, or removed at a distance from him; but it is an omnipresent, working will and desire, which is itself, the beginning and forming of the thing desired. Our own will, and desirous imagination, when they work and create in us a settled aversion, or fixed love of anything, resemble in some degree, the creating power of God, which makes things out of itself, or its own working desire. And our will, and working imagination could not have the power that it has now even after the fall, but because it is a product, or spark of that first divine will or desire which is omnipotent.

[App-1-44] 16. Here therefore we have plainly found the true original, or first source of all things. The desire of God is the first former, generator, and creator of all things; they are all the births of this omnipotent, working desire; for everything that comes into being, must have the nature of that power that formed it, and therefore the nature of every creature must stand in an attractive desire, that is, everything must be a created, attractive power; because it is the birth, or product of a desire, or attractive power, and could neither come into, nor continue in being, but because it was generated not only by, but out of an attracting desire. And herein lies the band, or knot of all created being and life.

[App-1-45] 17. Will or desire in the Deity, is justly considered as God the Father, who from eternity to eternity, wills or generates only the Son, from which eternal generating, the Holy Spirit eternally proceeds: and this is the infinite perfection or fullness of beatitude of the life of the Triune God.

[App-1-46] Now, as the unbeginning, eternal desire is in God, so is the created desire in the creature; it stands in the same tendency, hath the nature of the divine desire, because it is a branch out of it, or created from it. In the Deity, the eternal will or desire, is a desiring, or generating the Son, whence the Holy Spirit proceeds; the desire that is come out of God in the form of a creature, has the same tendency, it is a desire of the Son and Holy Spirit. And every created thing in heaven and earth attains its perfection, by its gaining in some degree, the birth of the Son and Holy Spirit of God in it: for all attraction and desire in the creature, generates in them as it did in God; and so the birth of the Son and Holy Spirit of God arises in some degree, or other, in all creatures that are in their proper state of perfection.

[App-1-47] 18. And here lies the ground of that plain, and most fundamental doctrine of scripture, that the Father is the creator, the Son the regenerator, and the Holy Spirit the sanctifier. For what is this but saying in the plainest manner, that as there are three in God, so there must be three in the creature, that as the three stand related to one another in God, so must they stand in the same relation in the creature. For if a threefold life of God must have distinct shares in the creation, blessing, and perfection of man, is it not a demonstration, that the life of man must stand in the same threefold state, and have such a Trinity in it, as has its true likeness to that Trinity which is in God?

[App-1-48] That which generates in God, must generate in the creature; and that which is generated in God, must be generated in the creature; and that which proceeds from this generation in the Deity, must proceed from this generation in the creature: and therefore, the same threefold life must be in the creature in the same manner as it is in God. For a creature that can only exist, and be blessed by the distinct operation of a Triune God upon it, must have the same Triune nature that is answerable to it. And herein lies our true, and easy, and sound, and edifying knowledge and belief of the mystery of a Trinity in Unity: and this is all that the scripture teaches us concerning it. It is not a doctrine that requires learned or nice speculations, in order to be rightly apprehended by us. But when with the scriptures, we believe the Father to be our creator, the Son our regenerator, and the Holy Spirit our sanctifier; then we are learned enough in this mystery, and begin to know the Triune God in the same manner in time, that we shall know him in eternity.

[App-1-49] And the reason why this great mystery of a Trinity in the Deity is thus revealed to us, and the necessity of a baptism in the Name of the Father, Son, and Holy Spirit, laid upon us, is this; it is to show us, that the divine, Triune life of God is lost in us, and that nothing less than a birth from the Son and Holy Spirit of God in us, can restore us to our first likeness to that Triune God, who at first created us. This I have fully shown in the little treatise upon regeneration.

[App-1-50] 19. When man was created in his original perfection, the Holy Trinity was his creator; the breath of lives, which became a living soul, was the breath of the Triune God: but when man began to will, and desire, that is, to generate contrary to the Deity, then the life of the Triune God extinguished in him.

[App-1-51] The desire of man being turned from God, lost the birth of the Son, and the proceeding of the Holy Spirit; and so fell into, or under the light and spirit of this world: that is, of a paradisaical man, enjoying union and communion with Father, Son, and Holy Ghost, and living on earth in such enjoyment of God, as the angels live in heaven, he became an earthly creature, subject to the dominion of this outward world, capable of all its evil influences, subject to its vanity and mortality; and as to his outward life, stood only in the highest rank of animals. This and this alone, is the true nature and degree of the fall of man; it was neither more nor less than this. It was a falling out of one world, or kingdom, into another, it was changing the life, Light and Spirit of God, for the light and spirit of this world. Thus it was that Adam died the very day of his transgression, he died to all the influences and operations of the kingdom of God upon him, as we die to the influences of this world, when the soul leaves the body; and, on the other hand, all the influences, operations and powers of the elements of this life became opened in him, as they are in every animal at its birth into this world.

[App-1-52] All other accounts of that fall, which only suppose the loss of some moral perfection, or natural acuteness of his rational powers, are not only senseless fictions, but are an express denial of the Old and New Testament account of it; for the Old Testament expressly says, that Adam was to die the day of his transgression, and therefore it is certain, that he then did die, and that the fall was his losing his first life: and to say that he did not die to that first life in which he was created, is the same denial of scripture, as to say, that he did not eat of the forbidden tree.

[App-1-53] Again, the same scripture assures us, that after the fall, his eyes were opened; I suppose this is a proof, that before the fall, they were shut. And what is this, but saying in the plainest manner, that before the fall, the life, light and spirit of this world, were shut out of him? and that the opening of his eyes, was only another way of saying, that the life and light of this world were opened in him?

[App-1-54] If an angel, or any inhabitant of heaven, was to be sent of a message into this world, it must be supposed, that neither the darkness, nor light of this world, could act according to their nature upon him; and therefore, though he was here, he must be said not to have the opened eyes of this world: but if this heavenly messenger should be taken with our manner of life, should be in doubts about returning to heaven, and long to have such flesh and blood as ours is, as earnestly as Adam longed to eat of the earthly tree; and if by this longing, he should actually obtain that which he desired; must it not then be said of him, when he had got this new nature, his eyes were opened, to see light and darkness; and that only for this reason, because the heavenly life was departed from him, and the earthly life of this world was opened in him? And thus it was that Adam died, and thus his eyes were opened.

[App-1-55] Again, when his eyes were thus opened, or the light and life of this world thus opened in him, he was immediately ashamed and shocked at the sight of his own body, and wanted to hide it from himself, and from the sight of the sun. Now, how could this have happened to him, if his body had not undergone some very extraordinary change, from a state of glory and perfection, to a lamentable degree of vileness and impurity?

[App-1-56] All the terror at his fallen state, seems to arise from the sad condition, in which he saw and felt his outward body. This made him ashamed of himself; this made him tremble, at hearing the voice of God; this made him creep behind the trees, and endeavor to hide and cover his body with leaves.

[App-1-57] And is not this the same thing, as if Adam had said, "All my sin, my guilt, my misery, and shame, is published before heaven and earth, by this sad state and condition in which my body now appears."

[App-1-58] But now, what was this sad state and condition of his body? What did Adam see in the manner and form of it that filled him with such confusion? Why, he only saw that he was fallen from his paradisaical glory, to have the same gross flesh and blood as the beasts and animals of this world have; which was, to bring forth an offspring in the same earthly manner, as they did. He could see, and be ashamed of no other deformity in his body, but that which he had in common with the animals of this world; and therefore there was nothing else in his outward form that he could be ashamed of; and yet it was his outward form that filled him with confusion. And is not this the greatest of all proofs, that before his fall, his body had not this nature and condition of the beasts in it? Is it not the same thing, as if he had said, "this body which now makes me ashamed, and which I want to hide, though it be only with thin leaves, because it brings me down amongst the animals of this world, is not that first body of glory into which God at first breathed the breath of lives, and in which I became a living soul."

[App-1-59] Again, if Adam's body had been of the same kind of flesh and blood as ours is now, only in a better state of health and vigor, how could he have been created immortal? If he was not created immortal, how can it be said, that sin alone brought mortality, or death into human nature? But if he had immortality in his first created state, then he must have such a body as none of the elements, or elementary things of this world could act upon; for there is no death in any creature of this world, but what is brought upon it by that strife and destruction which the four elements bring upon one another. But if sin alone gave the elements, and all elementary things their first power of acting upon the body of Adam; then it is plain, that before his sin, he had not, could not have a body of such flesh and blood as we now have, but that he stood, as to the state, nature, and condition of his outward body, at as great a distance and difference from the animals of this world, as heaven does from earth, and was created with flesh and blood as much exalted above, and superior to the nature and power of all the elements, as the beasts of this world are under them.

[App-1-60] And herein plainly appears the true sense of that saying, "God made not death," that is, he made not that which is mortal, or dying in the human nature, but sin alone formed and produced that in man, which could, and must die like the bodies of beasts. Death, and the grave, and the resurrection, are all standing proofs, that the body of bestial flesh and blood, which we now have, at the sight of which Adam was ashamed, which must die, which can rot in the grave, which must not be seen after the resurrection, was not that first body, in which Adam appeared before God in paradise: for it is an undeniable truth of scripture, that this flesh and blood cannot enter into the kingdom of God; it must be a truth of the same certainty, that this flesh and blood could not by God himself be brought into paradise; but that it must have the same original with every other polluted thing that is an abomination in his sight, or incapable of entering into the kingdom of God.

[App-1-61] 20. That the gospel also plainly shows, that man was created in the dignity and glorious enjoyment of the Triune life of God, and that his fall, was a falling into the earthly life of the light and spirit of this world, I have sufficiently proved from the greatest articles of the Christian faith, concerning the necessity, nature, and manner of our redemption, in the book of Christian Regeneration. I have there shown, that baptism in the Name of the Father, Son, and Holy Ghost, signifies nothing but our being born again into this Triune life of God. That the necessity of being born again of the Word or Son of God, of being born of the Spirit, or receiving him as a sanctifier of our newly raised nature, plainly proves that what we lost by the fall, was this Triune life of God: he that denies this, denies the whole of the Christian redemption. {See Spirit of Prayer, Part II, page 63, &c., page 91. Way to Divine Knowledge, pages 39-53.}

[App-1-62] 21. It has been already observed, that when man was created in his original perfection, the Holy Trinity was his creator; but when man was fallen, or had lost his first divine life, then there began a new language of a redeeming religion. Father, Son, and Holy Ghost were now to be considered, not as creating every man as they created the first, but as differently concerned in raising the fallen race of mankind, to that first likeness of the Holy Trinity in which their first father was created: hence it is, that the scriptures speak of the Father, as drawing, and calling men; because the desire which is from the Father's nature, must be the first mover, stirrer, and beginner. This desire must be moved and brought into an anguishing state, and have the agitation of a fire that is kindling; and then men are truly drawn by the Father.

[App-1-63] The Son of God is now considered as the regenerator or raiser of a new birth in us; because he enters a second time into the life of the soul, that his own nature and likeness may be again generated in it, and that he may be that to the soul in its state, which he is to the Father in the Deity.

[App-1-64] The Holy Ghost is represented as the sanctifier, or finisher of the divine life restored in us; because as in the Deity, the Holy Ghost proceeds from the Father and the Son, as the amiable, blessed finisher of the Triune life of God; so the fallen nature of man cannot be raised out of its unholy state, cannot be blessed and sanctified with its true degree of the divine life, till the Holy Spirit arises up in it.

[App-1-65] Since then the Triune God, or the three persons in the one God, must have this difference of shares, must reach out this different help to the raising up of fallen man, it is undeniable, that the first created man stood in the image and real likeness of the one God, not only representing, but really having in his birth and life, the birth and life of the Holy Trinity. God the Father, Son, and Holy Ghost had such a Unity in Trinity in man, as they had in the Deity itself: how else could man be the image and likeness of the Holy Trinity, if it was not such a birth in man, as it was in itself? Or, how could the Holy Trinity dwell and operate in man, each person according to its respective nature, unless there was the same threefold life in man as there is in God? How could the Holy Trinity be an object of man's worship and adoration, if the Holy Trinity had not produced itself in man? The creature is only to own and worship its creator; therefore Father, Son, and Holy Ghost must have each of them their creaturely offspring, or product in man, if man is to worship Father, Son, and Holy Spirit. If therefore you deny angels, and the souls of perfect men to have the triune nature, of life of God in them: if you deny that Father, Son, and Holy Spirit, have such union and relation in the soul, as they have out of it, you are guilty of as great heresy and apostasy from the gospel, as if you denied the Father to be the creator or him that calleth and draweth, the Son to be the redeemer, or him that regenerateth, and the Holy Spirit to be him that sanctifieth human nature.

[App-1-66] 22. Again: consider this great truth, which will much illustrate this matter; you can be an inhabitant of no world, or a partaker of its life, but by its being inwardly the birth of your own life, or by having the nature and condition of that world born in you. As thus, hell must be inwardly born in the soul, it must arise up within it, as it does without it, before the soul can become an inhabitant of it.

[App-1-67] Again: that which is the life of this outward world, viz., its fire, and light, and air, must have such a state and birth within you, as they have without you, before you can be an inhabitant or partaker of the life of this world; that is, fire must be in you, must be the same fire, have the same place and nature within you, have the same relation to the light and air that is within you, as it has without you, or else the fire of the outward world, cannot keep up, or have any communion with your own life.

[App-1-68] The light of this world can signify nothing to you, cannot reach or enrich you with its powers and virtues, if the same light is not arisen in the same manner in the kindling of your own life, as it arises in the outward world.

[App-1-69] The air also of this world can do you no good, can be no blower up and preserver of your life, but because it has the same birth in you, that it has in outward nature. And therefore it must be a truth of the greatest certainty, that so it must of all necessity be with respect to the kingdom of God, or that life which is to be had in the beatific presence of God; it must, by an absolute necessity, have the same birth within you, as it has without you, before you can enter into it, or become an inhabitant of it: if you are to live, and be eternally blessed in the triune life, or beatific presence of God, that triune life, must, of the utmost necessity, first make itself creaturely in you; it must be and arise in you, as it does without you, before you can possibly enter into any communion with it.

[App-1-70] Now is there anything more plain and scriptural, more easy to be conceived, more pious to be believed, and more impossible to be denied, than all this? And yet this is all that I have said, in two propositions in the treatise upon Christian Regeneration: it is there said, "Man was created by God after his own image, and in his own likeness, a living mirror of the divine nature; where Father, Son, and Holy Ghost each brought forth their own nature in a creaturely manner." Now, what is this, but saying, that the Holy Trinity brought forth a creature in its own likeness, standing in a creaturely birth of the divine, triune life? If it did not stand thus, how could it have its form or creation from the Holy Trinity? Or how could it without this triune life in itself, enter into, or be a partaker of the triune life or presence of God? In the next proposition it is said; "In it, that is, in this created image of the Holy Trinity, the Father's nature generated the divine Word, or Son of God, and the Holy Ghost proceeded from them both as an amiable, moving life of both. This was the likeness or image of God, in which the first man was created, a true offspring of God, in whom the divine birth sprung up as in the Deity, where Father, Son, and Holy Ghost, saw themselves in a creaturely manner."

[App-1-71] Now, what is this, but saying in the plainest manner, only thus much, that the triune, creaturely life stood in the same birth and generation of its threefold life, as the Deity doth, whose image, likeness, and offspring it is? And can it possibly be otherwise; for if the creature cometh from the Father, Son, and Holy Ghost, as their created image and likeness, must not that which it hath from the Father, be of the nature of the Father, that which it hath from the Son, be of the nature of the Son, and that which it hath from the Holy Ghost, be of the nature of the Holy Ghost? And must they not therefore stand in the creature in such relation to one another, as they do in the creator? If it is the nature of the Father to generate, if it is the nature of the Son to be generated, if it is the nature of the Holy Ghost to proceed from both, must not that which you have from the Father generate in you, that which you have from the Son be generated in you, and that which you have from the Holy Ghost, proceed from both in you? All which is only saying this plain and obvious truth, that that being, or created life, which you have from Father, Son, and Holy Ghost, must stand in such a triune relation within you as it does without you; that having this threefold likeness of God, you may be capable of entering into an enjoyment of his triune, beatific life or presence.

[App-1-72] For, consider again this instance, with regard to the life of this world. The fire, and light, and air, of outward nature, must become creaturely in you; that is, you must have a fire that is your own creaturely fire, you must have a light that is generated by, or from your own fire, a breath that proceeds from your own fire and light, as the air of outward nature proceeds from its fire and light: you must have all this nature and birth of fire, and light, and air in your own creaturely being, or you cannot possibly live in, or have a life from the fire, and light, and air of outward nature: no omnipotence can make you a partaker of the life of this outward world, without having the life of this outward world born in your own creaturely being. And therefore, no omnipotence can make you a partaker of the beatific life or presence of the Holy Trinity, unless that life stands in the same triune state within you, as it does without you.

[App-1-73] The nature of this world must become creatural in you, before you can live, or have a share in the life of this world; the triune nature of God must breathe forth itself to stand creaturely in you, before you can live, or have a share in the beatific life or presence of the triune God.

[App-1-74] Now, is not all this strictly according to the very outward letter, and inward truth of the most important articles of the Christian religion? For what else can be meant by the necessity of our being born again of the Word, or Son of God, being born of the Spirit of God, in order to our entrance into the kingdom of heaven? Is not this saying, that the triune life of God must first have its birth in us, before we can enter into the triune, beatific life, or presence of God? What else is taught us by that new birth sought for by a baptism, in the Name of the Father, Son, and Holy Ghost? Does it not plainly tell us, that the triune nature of the Deity is that which wants to be born in us, and that our redemption consists in nothing else but in the bringing forth this new birth in us, and that, being thus born again in the likeness of the Holy Trinity, we may be capable of its threefold blessing and happiness? The New Testament tells us of the impossibility of our being made holy, but by the Holy Spirit of God: now, how could we want any distinct thing particularly from the Son of God, any distinct thing, particularly from the Holy Ghost, in order to raise and repair our fallen nature, how could this particularity be thus absolutely necessary, but because the holy threefold life of the Deity must stand within us, in the birth of our own life, as it does without us, that so we may be capable of living in God, and God in us.

[App-1-75] Search to eternity, why no devil, or beast can possibly be a partaker of the kingdom of heaven, and there can only this one reason be assigned for it, because neither of them have the triune, holy life of God in them: for every created thing does, and must, and can only want, seek, unite with, and enjoy that outwardly, which is of the same nature with itself. Remove a devil where you will, he is still in hell, and always at the same distance from heaven; he can touch, or taste, or reach nothing but what is in hell. Carry a beast where you please, either to court, or to church, he is yet at the same infinite distance from the joys and fears either of church, or court, as the beasts that never saw anything else but their own kind: and all this is grounded solely on this eternal truth; namely, that no being can rise higher than its own life reaches. The circle of the birth of life in every creature is its necessary circumference, and it cannot possibly reach any further; and therefore it is a joyful truth, that beings created to worship and adore the Holy Trinity, and to enter into the beatific life and presence of the triune God, must, of all necessity, have the same triune life in their own creaturely being. And now, what can be so glorious, so edifying, so ravishing, as this knowledge of God and ourselves? The very thought of our standing in this likeness and relation to the infinite creator and being of all beings, is enough to kindle the divine life within us, and melt us into a continual love and adoration: for how can we enough love and adore that Holy Trinity which has created us in its own likeness, that we might live in an eternal union and communion with it? Will anyone call this an irreverent familiarity, or bold looking into the Holy Trinity, which is nothing else but a thankful adoration of it, as our glorious Father and creator? It is our best and only acknowledgement of the greatest truths of the holy scriptures; it is the scripture doctrine of the Trinity kept in its own simplicity, separated from scholastic speculations, where the three in God, are only distinguished by that threefold share that they have in the creation and redemption of man. When we thus know the Trinity in ourselves, and adore its high original in the Deity, we are possessed of a truth of the greatest moment, that enlightens the mind with the most solid and edifying knowledge, and opens to us the fullest understanding of all that concerns the creation, fall, and redemption of man.

[App-1-76] Without this knowledge, all the scripture will be used as a dead letter, and formed only into a figurative, historical system of things, that has no ground in nature; and learned divines can only be learned in the explication of phrases, and verbal distinctions.

[App-1-77] The first chapters of Genesis will be a knot that cannot be untied; the mysteries of the gospel will only be called federal rites, and their inward ground reproached as enthusiastic dreams; but when it is known, that the triune nature of God was brought forth in the creation of man, that it was lost in his fall, that it is restored in his redemption, a never-failing light arises in all scripture, from Genesis to the Revelation. Everything that is said of God, as Father, regenerator, or sanctifier of man; everything that is said of Jesus Christ, as redeeming, forming, dwelling in, and quickening; and of the Holy Spirit, as moving and sanctifying us: everything that is said of the holy sacraments, or promised in and by them, has its deep and inward ground fully discovered; and the whole Christian religion is built upon a rock, and that rock is nature, and God will appear to be doing every good to us, that the God of all nature can possibly do. The doctrine of the Holy Trinity is wholly practical; it is revealed to us, to discover our high original, and the greatness of our fall, to show us the deep and profound operation of the triune God in the recovery of the divine life in our souls; that by the means of this mystery thus discovered, our piety may be rightly directed, our faith and prayer have their proper objects, that the workings and aspirings of our own hearts may cooperate, and correspond with that triune life in the Deity, which is always desiring to manifest itself in us; for as everything that is in us, whether it be heaven, or hell, rises up in us by a birth, and is generated in us by the will-spirit of our souls, which kindles itself either in heaven, or hell; so this mystery of a triune Deity manifesting itself, as a Father creating, as a Son, or Word, regenerating, as a Holy Spirit sanctifying us, is not to entertain our speculation with dry, metaphysical distinctions of the Deity, but to show us from what a height and depth we are fallen, and to excite such a prayer and faith, such a hungering and thirsting after this triune fountain of all good, as may help to generate and bring forth in us that first image of the Holy Trinity in which we were created, and which must be born in us before we can enter into the state of the blessed: here we may see the reason, why the learned world has had so many fruitless disputes about this mystery, and why it has been so often a stone of stumbling to philosophers and critics; it is because they began to reason about that, which never was proposed to their reason, and which no more belongs to human learning and philosophy, than light belongs to our ears, or sounds to our eyes. No person has any fitness, nor any pretense, nor any ground from scripture, to think, or say anything of the Trinity, till such time as he stands in the state of the penitent returning prodigal, weary of his own sinful, shameful nature; and desiring to renounce the world, the flesh, and the devil, and then is he first permitted to be baptized into the Name of the Father, Son, and Holy Ghost: this is the first time the gospel teaches, or calls anyone to the acknowledgement of the Holy Trinity. Now, as this knowledge is first given in baptism, and there only as a signification of a triune life of the Deity, which must be regenerated in the soul; so the scriptures say nothing afterwards to this baptized penitent concerning the Trinity, but only with regard to regeneration, everywhere only showing him how Father, Son, and Holy Ghost, all equally divine, must draw, awaken, quicken, enlighten, move, guide, cleanse, and sanctify the new-born Christian: is it not therefore undeniably plain, that all abstract speculations of this mystery, how it is in itself, how it is to be ideally conceived, or scholastically expressed by us, are a wandering from that true light, in which the Trinity of God is set before us, which is only revealed as a key, or direction to the true depths of that regeneration, which is to be sought for from the triune Deity? But to go on in a further account of the creation.

[App-1-78] 23. Now, as all creatures, whether intellectual, animate, or inanimate, are products, or emanations of the divine desire, created out of the Father, who from eternity to eternity generates the Son, whence the Holy Spirit eternally proceeds; so every intelligent, created being, not fallen from its state, stands in the same birth, or generating desire, it generates in its degree, as God the Father generates eternally the Son, and is blessed and perfected in the divine life, by having the Holy Spirit arise up in it.

[App-1-79] Hence it is, that those angels which stood, and continued in the same will and desire in which they came out from God, willing and desiring as God from all eternity had willed and desired, were by the rising up of the Holy Spirit in them, confirmed and established in the divine life, and so became eternally and inseparably united with the ever-blessed triune Deity.

[App-1-80] On the other hand, those angels which did not keep their will and desire in its first created tendency, but raised up an own will and desire, which own will and desire was their direct, full choosing and desiring to be, and do something which they could not be, and do in God, and is therefore properly called their aspiring to be above God, or to be without any dependence upon him; these angels, by thus going backwards with their will and desire out of, or from God and the divine truth, could only find, or generate that which had the utmost contrariety to God and the divine birth, and so became under a necessity of finding themselves in an eternal state, spirit and life that was directly contrary to all that is good, holy, amiable, blessed and divine.

[App-1-81] Now, the will and desire in every creature is generating, and efficacious, strictly according to the state and nature of that creature; {See Way to Divine Knowledge, pages 139-160.} therefore, eternal beings in an eternal state, must have an eternal power and efficacy in the working of their wills and desires: when therefore those angels, with all the strength of their eternal desires, turned away from, and contrary to God and the divine birth, they could become nothing else, but beings eternally separated and broken off from all that was God and goodness: for eternal beings that stood only in an eternal state, acting with all their vigor, not doubting, but strongly willing, could not do anything that had only a temporal nature and effect, because they stood not in such a nature or such a world, and therefore what they willed and generated with all their nature, (which was a contrariety to God) that became the eternal state of their nature. And this is the birth and origin of hellish beings.

[App-1-82] God had done all to them and for them, that he had done to and for the angels that stood; he had given them the same holy beginning of their lives, had brought them forth out of himself in the same tendency, that which was the nature of other angels, was theirs; he could not make any established, fixed, and unchangeable angels, because the life of everything must be a birth, and willing beings must have a birth of their wills; he could not make them fixed, because everything that comes from God, must so come from him, as it was in him, a self- existent and self-moving power, and therefore no goodness of God could hinder their having a self-motion, because they were, and could be nothing else but creatures brought forth by, and out of his own self- existent and self-moving nature.

[App-1-83] God is all good, and everything that comes out from him, as his creature, product, or offspring, must come forth in that state of goodness, which it had in him; and every creature, however high in its birth from God, must in the beginning of its life, have a power of joining with or departing from God, because the beginning of its life is nothing else but the beginning of its own self-motion as a creature; and therefore no creature can have its state or condition fixed, till it gives itself up either wholly unto God, or turns wholly from him; for if it is an intelligent creature, it can only be so, by having the intelligent will of God derived into it, or made creaturely in it; but the intelligent will brought into a creaturely form, must be that which it was in the creator, and therefore must be the same self-existent and self-moving power that it was before it became creaturely in any angel or spirit. And thus the cause and origin of evil, wherever it is, is absolutely and eternally separated from God.

[App-1-84] 24. Again: as all intelligent beings can no way attain their happiness and perfection, but by standing with their will and desire united to God, in the same tendency in which the Father eternally generateth the Son, from whence the Holy Spirit proceedeth as the finisher of the triune, beatific life, so the same thing is manifestly proved to us by the lowest kind of beings that are in this visible world; for all vegetables, by their attraction or astringency, which is their desire, and is an outbirth of the divine desire, reach their utmost perfection by the same progress, that is, by getting a birth of the light and spirit of this outward world into them, and so become infallible, though remote proofs that no life can be brought to its proper perfection in the creature, till the image of the triune life of God, is, according to the state and capacity of the creature, formed in it: look where you will, everything proclaims and proves this great truth. The Christian doctrine of the salvation of mankind by a birth of the Son, and Holy Spirit of God in them, is not only written in scripture, but in the whole state and frame of nature, and of every life in this world; for every perfect fruit openly declares, that it can have no goodness in it, till the light and spirit of this world has done that to it and in it, which the Light and Spirit of God must do to the soul of man, and therefore is a full proof, that it is absolutely necessary for every human creature to desire, believe, and receive the birth of the Son and Holy Spirit of God to save it from its own wrath and darkness, as it is necessary for every fruit of the earth to be raised and regenerated from its own bitterness and sourness, by receiving the light and spirit of this world into it.

[App-1-85] 25. Some learned men, willing to discover the image of the Holy Trinity in the creation, have observed three properties both in body and spirit, which they supposed to be a proper likeness of the Trinity. But all this is nothing to the matter.

[App-1-86] For as the Holy Trinity is a threefold life in God, so the image of the Trinity is only found in a threefold life in the creature; for it is the whole birth, or generation of the thing itself, whether it be corporeal or spiritual, that stands in such a threefold state as the Holy Trinity doth, that is the proper likeness or image of the Trinity. As there is one infinitely perfect Deity, because this one Deity is Father, Son, and Holy Spirit, so every creature that is an original production of the Deity, or in its proper state of perfection, stands in its whole being, or generating as the Deity doth, and neither hath, nor ever can have any perfection, but because the triune nature of God is manifested and brought forth in it; for perfection of life is God, and a perfection of life derived from God, must stand in the same threefold state, and that which is a life from the Deity, must have a life of the Trinity in it.

[App-1-87] 26. Take away attraction, or desire from the creature of this world, and you annihilate the creature; for where there is no attraction or desire, there can be no nature or being; and therefore attraction or desire shows the work of the creator in everything, or what is meant by the divine fiat, or creating power. Now, what is it which this attraction or desire wants, hungers, draws and reaches after? Nothing else but the light and spirit of this world. What is the true, deep, and infallible ground of this? Why does this desire thus work in every life of this world? It is because the eternal will in the Deity, is a desiring or generating the Son, from whence the Holy Spirit of God proceeds: and therefore attraction, which is an outbirth of the divine desire, stands in a perpetual desiring of the light and spirit of this world, because they are the two outbirths of the Light and Holy Spirit of God. What rational mind can help being charmed with this wonderful harmony and relation betwixt God, nature, and creature?

[App-1-88] 27. And now, my dear reader, if you are either Arian, or Deist, be so no longer: the ground is dug up from under you, and neither opinion has anything left to stand upon; you may wrangle and wrest the doctrine of scripture, because it is only taught in words; but the veil is now taken off from nature, and every plant and fruit will teach you with the clearness of a noonday sun, these two great truths; first, that Father, Son, and Holy Spirit are one being, one life, one God: secondly, that the soul, which is dead to the paradisaical life, must be made alive again by the birth of the Son and Holy Spirit of God in it, in the same manner as a dead seed is, and only can be brought to life in this world, by the light and spirit of this world.

[App-1-89] If you are an Arian, don't content yourself with the numbers that are with you, or with a learned name or two that are on your side: Arianism has never yet been recommended by the genius and learning of a Baronious, or Bellarmin; and nothing but a poor, groping, purblind philosophy, that is not able to look either at God, nature, or creature, hath ever led any man into it: for it is a truth proclaimed by all nature and creature, that there is a threefold life in God, and everything that is, whether it be happy, or miserable, perfect or imperfect, is only so, because it has, or has not the triune nature of God in it.

[App-1-90] A beginning fruit is like a poison; a seed, for a while, is shut up in a hard death. Why are they both at first in this state? It is because each of them stands as yet only in that first birth of nature, which is but a beginning manifestation of the Deity. Let the light of the sun, and the spirit of this world be born in them, and then the sour, astringent fruit, and the dead seed becomes a perfect, vegetable life, and is in its kind perfect, for this one only reason, because the triune life of the Deity is truly manifested in it.

[App-1-91] 28. If you are a Deist, made so, either by the disorderly state of your own heart, or by prejudices taken from the corruptions and divisions of Christians, or from a dislike of the language of scripture, or from an opinion of the sufficiency of a religion of human reason, or from whatever else it may be, look well to yourself, Christianity is no fiction of enthusiasm, or invention of priests.

[App-1-92] If you can show, that the gospel proposes to bring men into the kingdom of heaven by any other method, than that, which nature requires to make any creature a living member of this world, then I will acknowledge the gospel not to be founded in nature.

[App-1-93] But if what the gospel saith of the absolute necessity, that the fallen soul be born again of the Son and Holy Spirit of God, is the very same which all temporal nature saith of everything that is to enter into the life of this world, viz., that it cannot partake of the life of this world, till the light and spirit of this world is born in it; then does not all nature in this world, and every life in it, declare, that the Christian method of salvation is as necessary to raise fallen man, as the sun and spirit of this world is, to bring a creature alive into it?

[App-1-94] Now, as there is but one God, so there is but one nature, as unalterable as that God from whom it arises, and whose manifestation it is; so also there is but one religion founded in nature, and but one salvation possible in nature. Revealed religion is nothing else but a revelation of the mysteries of nature, for God cannot reveal, or require anything by a spoken or written word, but that which he reveals and requires by nature; for nature is his great book of revelation, and he that can only read its capital letters, will have found so many demonstrations of the truth of the written revelation of God. {Spirit of Love, Part II, pages 134-149.}

[App-1-95] But to show, that there is but one salvation possible in nature, and that possibility solely contained in the Christian method: look from the top to the bottom of all creatures, from the highest to the lowest beings, and you will find, that death has but one nature in all worlds, and in all creatures: look at life in an angel, and life in a vegetable, and you will find, that life has but one and the same form, one and the same ground in the whole scale of beings: no omnipotence of God can make that to be life, which is not life, or that to be death, which is not death, according to nature; and the reason is, because nature is nothing else but God's own outward manifestation of what he inwardly is, and can do; and therefore no revelation from God can teach, or require anything but that which is taught and required by God in, and through nature. The mysteries of religion therefore, are no higher, nor deeper than the mysteries of nature, and all the rites, laws, ceremonies, types, institutions and ordinances given by God from Adam to the apostles, are only typical of something that is to be done, or instrumental to the doing of that, which the unchangeable working of nature requires to be done. As sure therefore as there is but one and the same thing that is death, and one and the same thing that is life throughout all nature, whether temporal or eternal, so sure is it, that there is but one way to life or salvation for fallen man. And this way, let it be what it will, must and can be only that, which has its reason and foundation in that one universal nature, which is the one unchangeable manifestation of the Deity. For if there is but one thing that is life, and one thing that is death throughout all nature, from the highest angel to the hardest flint upon earth, then it must be plain, that the life which is to be raised or restored by religion, must, and can only be restored according to nature: and therefore, true religion can only be the religion of nature, and divine revelation can do nothing else, but reveal and manifest the demands and workings of nature.

[App-1-96] 29. Now, the one great doctrine of the Christian religion and which includes all the rest, is this, that Adam, by his sin, died to the kingdom of heaven, or that the divine life extinguished within him; that he cannot be redeemed, or restored to this first divine life, but by having it kindled or regenerated in him by the Son and Holy Spirit of God: now, that which is here called death, his losing the Light and Spirit of the kingdom of heaven, and that which is here made necessary to make him alive again to the kingdom of heaven, is that very same which is called, and is death and life throughout all nature, both temporal and eternal: and therefore, the Christian religion requiring this method of raising man to a divine life, has its infallible proof from all nature. {Spirit of Love, Part II, page 117, &c.} Consider death, or the deadness that is in a hard flint, and you will see what is the eternal death of a fallen angel: the flint is dead, or in a state of death, because its fire is bound, compacted, shut up, and imprisoned; this is its chains and bands of death: a steel struck against a flint will show you, that every particle of the flint consists of this compacted fire.

[App-1-97] Now, a fallen angel is in no other state of death, knows no other death than this: it is in its whole spiritual, intelligent being, nothing else, but that very same which the flint is, in its insensible materiality, viz., an imprisoned compacted, darkened fire-spirit, shut up, and tied in its own chains of darkness, as the fire of the flint; and you shall see by and by, that the flint is changed from its first state into its present hardness of death, in the same manner, and by the same means, as the heavenly angel is become a fiery serpent in the state of eternal death.

[App-1-98] Now, look at every death that can be found betwixt that of a fallen angel, and that of a hard flint, and you will find that death enters nowhere, into no kind of vegetable, plant, or animal, but as it has entered into the angel, and the flint, and stands in the same manner in everything wherever it is.

[App-1-99] Now, that a fallen angel, is nothing else but a fire-spirit imprisoned in the same manner as a flint is an imprisoned fire, is plain from the scripture account of them; not only because all the wrathful properties of a fire without light, are ascribed to them as their essential qualities, but because the place of their habitation, or the state of their life, is a fire of hell. For how could it be possible, that a hellish fire should be the eternal state of their life, unless their nature was such a fire? Must not their painful condition arise from their nature, and their misery be only a sensibility of themselves, of that which they have made themselves to be? Therefore, if fire shut up in darkness, is the nature of hell, it can only be so, because such a darkened fire is the very nature of a fallen angel. Or how again could the human soul, which has withstood its salvation in this life, be said to fall into eternal death, or the fire of hell, if the soul itself did not become that fire of hell? For when you say the soul enters into hell, you say neither more nor less, than if you had said, that hell enters into the soul; therefore, the state of hell, and the state of the soul in hell, is one and the same thing. If therefore hell is a state of fire shut up, and imprisoned from all communion with light, then the same dark, imprisoned fire must be the nature of the fallen angel and lost soul; and thus, what your eyes see to be the death or deadness of a flint, is that same thing, or that same state of the thing, which the scripture assures you, to be the eternal death of a fallen angel, and a lost soul. Here also you may see a plain proof of what I have elsewhere declared in it, or the in-spoken Word of life given to Adam at his fall, it is in itself, as a fallen soul, the same dark, fiery spirit, as the devils are; and that the reason why men wholly given up to wickedness, and who have suppressed the redeeming power of God in their souls, do not become fully sensible of this state of their souls, is this, because the soul, while it is in this flesh and blood, is capable of being softened, assuaged, and comforted in some degree or other, by the influences of the sun and spirit of this world, as all other creatures and beings are. And if it was not thus, how could it be a plain, constant doctrine of scripture, that when the unredeemed soul departs this life, it is incapable of anything but hell? Is not this directly saying, that hell, or the sensibility of hell was only hid and suppressed in such a soul, by the life and light of this world shining upon it.

[App-1-100] Now what I have said of the sad condition of the soul at the fall, that it lost the divine life, or the birth of the Son and Holy Spirit of God in it, and so became the same dark, fiery nature, as the devils, is not possible to be denied, without denying the most universally received doctrine of scripture.

[App-1-101] Is it not a fundamental doctrine of scripture, that Adam and all his posterity had been left in a state of eternal death, or damnation, unless Jesus Christ had become their redeemer, and taken them out of their natural state? But how can you believe, or own they had been left in this state, without believing and owning that they were in it? Or, how can you with the scripture believe, that by the fall they became heirs of eternal death and damnation with the devils, unless you believe and affirm, that by the fall they became of a hellish, diabolical nature? Or how can you hold, that by the fall they wanted to be delivered from the state of the devils, and yet not allow, that by the fall, they got the nature of the devils? Can anything be more absurd and inconsistent? Is it not the same thing as saying, that God made them heirs of eternal death and hell, before they were by nature fit for it, or before they had extinguished in themselves the divine life which was at first brought forth in them.

[App-1-102] Again: it is a scripture doctrine of the utmost certainty and importance, that those souls which have totally resisted and withstood all that God has done in them and for them by his

Son Jesus Christ, will, at their departure from the body, be incapable of anything but eternal death, or a hellish condition. Now, how can you possibly hold this doctrine of scripture, without holding at the same time, that the soul was in that state by the fall, before it had received its redeemer, as it is then in, when it has refused to receive him; for all that you can say of a lost soul is only this, that it has lost its redeemer, and therefore is only in the condition of that soul which has not received him: and therefore, if a lost soul is only an unredeemed soul, it must be plain, that the soul, before it had received its redeemer, was in the miserable condition, and had the miserable nature of a lost soul; and therefore, the only difference between the fallen soul, and the lost soul is this, they are both in the same need of a savior, both have the same miserable nature, because they have him not; but the one has the offer of him, and the other has refused to accept of him: but this final refusal of him, has only left him in possession of that fallen state of a hellish condition, which it had before a savior was given to it; and therefore, it is a truth of the utmost certainty, that Adam, by his fall, died to the divine life, and that by this death, his soul became of the same nature and condition with the fallen angels; and that therefore that new birth or regeneration, which he is to obtain by his redeemer Jesus Christ, is nothing else but the bringing back his soul into the kingdom of heaven, by a birth of the Son and the Holy Spirit of God brought forth in it, that so the life of the triune God may be in him again, as it was at his creation, when his soul was first breathed forth from the triune God. Is there anything more great, more glorious, or more consistent than these truths? Or is there any possibility of denying any part of them, without giving up the whole? Or is there any reason, why a Christian should be loath to believe this, and this alone, to be the true state of that regeneration which is so absolutely required by the gospel? Is it an unreasonable or uncomfortable thing to be told, that our regeneration is a true and real regaining that heavenly, divine, immortal life which at first came forth from God, and which alone can enter into the kingdom of heaven?

[App-1-103] Say that Adam did not die a real death at his transgression, that he did not lose a divine, immortal life, light and spirit, that he did not then first become a mere earthly, mortal, diabolical animal in the true and proper sense of the words, but that these things could only be affirmed of him in a figurative form of speech; say this, and then tell me what reality you have left in any article of our salvation?

[App-1-104] But if all these things must be said of fallen man according to the strictest truth of the expression, then the gospel regeneration, by a birth of the Son and Holy Spirit of God, arising a second time, in the soul of man, must mean such a real birth of a new heavenly life, as the proper sense of the words denote.

[App-1-105] 30. But to return now to my argumentation with the Deist.

[App-1-106] I have plainly shown you, that there is, and can be but one kind of death through all nature, whether temporal or eternal; and this I have done, by showing that eternal death in an angel, is the same thing, and has the same nature, as the hard death that is in a senseless flint. But if it be a certain truth, that death has but one way of entering into, or possessing any being from the highest of spiritual to the lowest of material creatures, then, though nothing else could be offered, it must be an infallible consequence, that life has but one way of being kindled throughout all nature, and that therefore there can be but one true religion, and that only can be it, which hath the one only way of kindling the heavenly life in the soul.

[App-1-107] Now, look where you will, the birth or kindling of life through all nature shows you, that the way of gospel regeneration, or raising the divine life again in the fallen soul, is that one and the same way, by which every kind of life is, and must be raised, wherever it is found. The gospel saith, unless the fallen soul be born again from above, be born again of the Word, or Son, and the Spirit of God, it cannot see, or enter into the kingdom of heaven: now here it says a truth, as much confirmed and ratified by all nature, as when it is said, except a creature hath the light and spirit of this world born in it, it cannot become a living animal of this world: or, except a seed have the light and spirit of this world incorporated in it, it cannot become a vegetable of this world, either as plant, fruit, or flower. Ask now wherein lies the absolute impossibility, that the fallen soul should be raised to its divine life, without a birth of the Son and Holy Spirit of God in it, and the true ground of this impossibility is only this, because a seed shut up in its own cold hardness, cannot possibly be raised into its highest vegetable life, but by a birth of the light and spirit of this world rising up in it.

[App-1-108] On the other hand, ask why a seed cannot possibly become a vegetable life, till the light and spirit of this world has been incorporated, or generated in it; and the only true ground of it is, because a fallen soul can only be raised to a divine life, or become a plant of the kingdom of heaven, by receiving the birth of the Light and Spirit of God into it. For the true reason, why life is in such a form, and rises in such a manner in the lowest creature living, is because it does, and must arise in the same manner, and stand in the same form in the highest of living creatures: for nature does, and must always act and generate in one and the same unchangeable manner, because it is nothing else but the manifestation of one unchangeable God.

[App-1-109] It is one and the same operation of light and spirit, that turns fire into every degree and kind of life that can be found either in temporal or eternal nature: it is one and the same operation of light and spirit, that upon one state of fire, raises an animal life, upon another state of fire, raises an intellectual and angelical life.

[App-1-110] There is no state or form of death in any creature, but where some kind of fire is shut up from light and spirit, nor is there any kind of life but what is kindled by the same operation of light and spirit upon some sort of fire.

[App-1-111] A fruit must first stand in a poisonous, sour, astringent, bitter, and fiery agitation of all its parts, before the light and spirit of this world can be generated in it. And thus light and spirit operate upon one sort of fire in the production of a vegetable life.

[App-1-112] An animal must be conceived in the same manner, it must begin in the same poison, and when nature is in its fiery strife, the light and spirit of this world kindles up the true animal life.

[App-1-113] Thus also there is but one kind, or state of death that can fall upon any creature, which is nothing else, but its losing the birth of light and spirit in itself, by which it becomes an imprisoned, dark fire. In an animal, vegetable, or mere matter, it is a senseless state of imprisoned fire; in an angel, or intellectual being, as the soul of man, it is a self- tormenting, self-generating, fiery worm, that cannot lose its sensibility, but is in a state of eternal death, because it is separated eternally from that light and spirit, which alone can raise a divine life in any intellectual creature.

[App-1-114] And thus it is plain, beyond all possibility of doubt, that there is neither life nor death to be found in any part of the creation but what sets its infallible seal to this gospel truth, that fallen man cannot enter into the kingdom of heaven any other way, than by being born again of the Son and Holy Spirit of God.

[App-1-115] 31. And here, my friend, you may with certainty see what a poor, groundless fiction, your religion of human reason is; its insignificancy and emptiness is shown you by everything you can look upon.

[App-1-116] Salvation is a birth of life, but reason can no more bring forth this birth, than it can kindle life in a plant, or animal: you might as well write the word "flame," upon the outside of a flint, and then expect that its imprisoned fire should be kindled by it, as to imagine, that any images, or ideal speculations of reason painted in your brain, should raise your soul out of its state of death, and kindle the divine life in it. No: would you have fire from a flint; its house of death must be shaken, and its chains of darkness broken off by the strokes of a steel upon it. This must of all necessity be done to your soul, its imprisoned fire must be awakened by the sharp strokes of steel, or no true light of life can arise in it: all nature and creature tells you, that the heavenly life must begin in you from the same causes, and the same operation as every earthly life, whether vegetable, or animal, does in this world. {Way to Divine Knowledge, page 162. &c.}

[App-1-117] Now, look where you will, all life must be generated in this manner: first, an attraction, or an astringing desire, must work itself into an anguishing agitation, or painful strife; this attraction become restless, and highly agitated, is that first poison, or strife of the properties of nature, which is and must be the beginning of every vegetable or animal life; it is by this strife, or inward agitation, that it reaches and gets a birth of the light and spirit of this world into it, and so becomes a living member, either of the animal or vegetable world.

[App-1-118] Now, this must be your process, a desire brought into an anguishing state; or the bitter sorrows and fiery agitations of repentance, must be the beginning of a divine life in your soul; 'tis by this awakened fire, or inward agitation, that it becomes capable of being regenerated, or turned into an heavenly life, by the Light and Holy Spirit of God.

[App-1-119] Nothing is, or can possibly be salvation, but this regenerated life of the soul: how vain and absurd would it be, to talk of a creature's being made a member of a vegetable or animal kingdom, through an outward grace or favor? or by any outward thing of any kind? For does not sense, reason, and all nature force you to confess, that it is absolutely impossible for anything to become a living member of the animal or vegetable kingdom, but by having the animal or vegetable life raised or brought forth in it? Therefore, does not sense and reason, and all nature join with the gospel in affirming, that no man can enter into the kingdom of heaven, till the heavenly life, or that which is the life in heaven, be born in him?

[App-1-120] The gospel says to the fallen, earthly man, that he must be born again from above, before he can see, enter into, or become a living member of the kingdom that is above.

[App-1-121] Now, he that understands this to be a figurative saying, that requires no real birth of a real life that is only above, but that an earthly man may enter into the life of heaven, by only carrying this figurative saying along with him, is as absurd, as ignorant, and offends as much against sense, reason, and all nature, as he who holds, that it is a figurative expression, when we say that nothing can enter into the vegetable kingdom, till it has the vegetable life in it, or be a member of the animal kingdom, till it hath the animal life born in it. {Way to Divine Knowledge, page 159.}

[App-1-122] And if some learned men will say, that it is religious enthusiasm to place our salvation, or capacity for the kingdom of heaven in the inward life or birth of heaven derived into our souls, they are only as learned as those who should call it philosophical enthusiasm to place the true nature of a vegetable, or animal, in its getting the inward, real birth of a vegetable and animal life. But to return to the Deist.

[App-1-123] You act as if God was a being that had an arbitrary, discretionary will, or wisdom, like that of a great prince over his subjects, who will reward mankind according as their services appeared to him. And so you fancy, that your religion of reason may appear as valuable as a religion that consists of forms, and modes, ordinances, and doctrines of revelation; but your idea of the last judgment is a fiction of reason that knows nothing rightly of God. God's last rewarding, is only his last separating everything into its own eternal place; it is only putting an end to all temporary nature, to the mixture of good and evil that is in time and leaving everything to be that in eternity, which it has made itself to be in time. Thus it is that our works follow us, and thus God rewards every man according to his deeds. {Way to Divine Knowledge, pages 169-183.}

[App-1-124] During the time of this world, God may be considered as the good husbandman; he sows the seed, the end of the world is the harvest, the angels are the reapers; if you are wheat, you are to be gathered into the barn, if you are tares, it signifies nothing, whence, or how, or by what means you are become so; tares are to be rejected, because they are tares, and wheat is to be gathered by the angels, because it is wheat: this is the mercy, and goodness, and discretionary justice of God that you are to expect at the last day. If you are not wheat, that is, if the heavenly life, or the kingdom of God, is not grown up in you it signifies nothing what you have chosen in the stead of it, or why you have chosen it, you are not that, which alone can help you to a place in the divine granary.

[App-1-125] God wants no services of men to reward, he only wants to have such a life quickened and raised up in you, as may make it possible for you to enter into, and live in heaven.

[App-1-126] He has created you out of his own eternal nature, and therefore you must have either an eternal life, or eternal death according to it. If eternal nature standeth in you, as it doth without you, then you are born again to the kingdom of heaven; but if nature works contrary in you to what it does in heaven, then you are in eternal death: and here lies the necessity of our being born again of the Word and Spirit of God, in order to the kingdom of heaven. It is because we are created out of that eternal nature which is the kingdom of heaven; 'tis because we are fallen out of it into a life of temporal nature, and therefore must have the life of eternal nature re-kindled in us, before we can possibly enter into the kingdom of heaven: therefore, look where you will, or at what you will, there is only one thing to be done, we want nothing else, but to have the light world, or the life of eternal nature kindled again in our souls, that life, and light, and spirit may be that in our souls, which they are in eternal nature, out of which our souls were created; that so we may be heavenly plants growing up to the kingdom of heaven. {Way to Divine Knowledge, pages 186-195.}

[App-1-127] You deceive yourself with fancied notions of the goodness of God; you imagine, that so perfect a being cannot damn you for so small a matter, as choosing a religion according to your own notions, or for not joining yourself with this, or that religious society.

[App-1-128] But all this is great ignorance of God, and nature, and religion. God has appointed a religion, by which salvation is to be had according to the possibility of nature, where no creature will be saved, or lost, but as it works with, or contrary to nature. For as the God of nature cannot himself act contrary to nature, because nature is the manifestation of himself, so every creature having its life in, and from nature, can have only such a life, or such a death as is according to the possibility of nature: and therefore, no creature will be saved, by an arbitrary goodness of God, but because of its conformity to nature, nor any creature lost by a want of compassion in God, but because of its salvation being impossible, according to the whole state of nature.

[App-1-129] It is not for notional, or speculative mistakes, that man will be rejected by God at the last day, or for any crimes that God could overlook, if he was so pleased; but because man has continued in his unregenerate state, and has resisted and suppressed that birth of life, by which alone he could become a member of the kingdom of heaven. The goodness and love of God have no limits or bounds, but such as his omnipotence hath: and everything that hath a possibility of partaking of the kingdom of heaven, will infallibly find a place in it.

[App-1-130] God comes not to judgment to display any wrath of his own, or to inflict any punishment as from himself upon man: he only comes to declare, that all temporary nature is at an end, and that therefore, all things must be, and stand in their own places in eternal nature: his sentence of condemnation, is only a leaving them that are lost, in such a misery of their own nature, as has finally rejected all that was possible to relieve it.

[App-1-131] You fancy that God will not reject you at the last day, for having not received this, or that mode, or kind of religion: but here all is mistake again. You might as well imagine, that no particular kind of element was necessary to extinguish fire, or that water can supply the place of air in kindling it, as suppose that no particular kind of religion is absolutely necessary to raise up such a divine life in the soul as can only be its salvation; for nature is the ground of all creatures, it is God's manifestation of himself, it is his instrument in, and by which he acts in the production and government of every life; and therefore a life that is to belong to this world, must be raised according to temporal nature, and a life that is to live in the next world, must be raised according to eternal nature.

[App-1-132] Therefore, all the particular doctrines, institutions, mysteries, and ordinances of a revealed religion that comes from the God of nature, must have their reason, foundation, and necessity in nature; and then your renouncing such a revealed religion, is renouncing all that the God of nature can do to save you.

[App-1-133] When I speak of nature as the true ground and foundation of religion, I mean nothing like that which you call the religion of human reason, or nature; for I speak here of eternal nature, which is the nature of the kingdom of heaven, or that eternal state, where all redeemed souls must have their eternal life, and live in eternal nature by a life derived from it, as men and animals live in temporal nature, by a life derived from it; for, seeing man stands with his soul in eternal nature, as certainly as he lives outwardly in temporal nature, and seeing man can have nothing in this world, neither happiness, nor misery from it, but what is according to the eternal nature of that world; and therefore, it is an infallible truth, that that particular religion can alone do us any good, or help us to the happiness of the next world, which works with, and according to eternal nature, and is able to generate that eternal life in us. But your notion of a goodness of God that may be expected at the last day, is as groundless, as if you imagined, that God would then stand over his creatures in a compassionate kind of weighing or considering who should be saved, and who damned, because a good-natured prince might do so towards variety of offenders.

[App-1-134] But hear how the God of nature himself speaks of this matter: Behold, I have set before thee, life and death, fire and water. choose whither thou wilt. Here lies the whole of the divine mercy; 'tis all on this side the day of judgment: till the end of time, God is compassionate and long-suffering, and continues to every creature a power of choosing life or death, water or fire; but when the end of time is come, there is an end of choice, and the last judgment is only a putting everyone into the full and sole possession of that which he has chosen.

[App-1-135] But your notion of a goodness of God at the last day supposes, that if a man has erroneously chosen death instead of life, fire instead of water, that God will not suffer such a creature to be deprived of salvation through a mistaken choice; but that in such a creature, he will make death to be life, and fire to be water. But you might as well expect that God should make a thing to be, and not to be at the same time; for this is as possible as to make hell to be heaven, or death to be life: for darkness can no more be light, death can no more be life, fire can no more be water in any being through a compassion of God towards it, than a circle could be a square, a falsehood a truth, or two to be more than three, by God's looking upon them.

[App-1-136] 32. Our salvation is an entrance into the kingdom of heaven: now, the life, Light and Spirit of heaven must as necessarily be in a creature before it can live in heaven, as the life, light and spirit of this world must be in a creature before it can live in this world: therefore the one only religion that can save any one son of fallen Adam, must be that which can raise, or regenerate the life, Light and Spirit of heaven in his soul, that when the light and spirit of this world leaves him, he may not find himself in eternal death and darkness.

[App-1-137] Now if this Light and Spirit of heaven is generated in your soul as it is generated in heaven, if it arises up in your nature within you, as it does in eternal nature without you, (which is the Christian new birth, or regeneration) then you are become capable of the kingdom of heaven, and nothing can keep you out of it; but if you die without this birth of the eternal Light and Spirit of God, then your soul stands in the same distance from, and contrariety to the kingdom of heaven, as hell does: if you die in this unregenerate state, it signifies nothing how you have lived, or what religion you have owned, all is left undone that was to have saved you: it matters not what form of life you have appeared in, what a number of decent, engaging or glorious exploits you have done either as a scholar, a statesman, or a philosopher; if they have proceeded only from the light and spirit of this world, they must die with it, and leave your soul in that eternal darkness, which it must have, so long as the Light and Spirit of eternity is not generated in it.

[App-1-138] And this is the true ground and reason, why an outward morality, a decency and beauty of life and conduct with respect to this world, arising only from a worldly spirit, has nothing of salvation in it: he that has his virtue only from this world, is only a trader of this world, and can only have a worldly benefit from it. For it is an undoubted truth, that everything is necessarily bounded by, or kept within the sphere of its own activity; and therefore, to expect heavenly effects from a worldly spirit, is nonsense: as water cannot rise higher in its streams, than the spring from whence it cometh, so no actions can ascend further in their efficacy, or rise higher in their value, than the spirit from whence they proceed. The spirit that comes from heaven is always in heaven, and whatsoever it does, tends to, and reaches heaven: the spirit that arises from this world, is always in it; it is as worldly when it give alms, or prays in the church, as when it makes bargains in the market. When therefore the gospel saith, he that gives alms to be seen of men, hath his reward; it is grounded on this general truth, that everything, every shape, or kind or degree of virtue that arises from the spirit of this world, has nothing to expect but that which it can receive from this world: for every action must have its nature, and efficacy according to the spirit from whence it proceeds. He that loves to see a crucifix, a worthless image, solely from this principle, because from his heart he embraces Christ as his suffering Lord and pattern, does an action poor, and needless in itself, which yet by the spirit from whence it proceeds, reaches heaven, and helps to kindle the heavenly life in the soul. On the other hand, he that from a selfish heart, a worldly spirit, a love of esteem, distinguishes himself by the most rational virtues of an exemplary life, has only a piety that may be reckoned amongst the perishable things of this world.

[App-1-139] 33. You (the Deist) think it a partiality unworthy of God, when you hear that the salvation of mankind is attributed and appropriated to faith and prayer in the Name of Jesus Christ. It must be answered, first, that there is no partiality of any kind in God; everything is accepted by him according to its own nature, and receives all the good from him that it can possibly receive: secondly, that a morality of life, not arising from the power and Spirit of Jesus Christ, but brought forth by the spirit of this world, is the same thing, has the same nature and efficacy in a heathen, as a Christian, does only the same worldly good to the one, as it does to the other; therefore, there is not the least partiality in God, with respect to the moral works of mankind, considered as arising from, and directed by the spirit of this world.

[App-1-140] Now, were these the only works that man could do, could he only act from the spirit of this world, no flesh could be saved, that is, no earthly creature, such as man is, could possibly begin to be of a heavenly nature, or have a heavenly life brought forth in him; so it is only a Spirit from heaven derived into the fallen nature, that makes any beginning of a heavenly life in it, that can lay the possibility of its having the least ability, tendency, and disposition towards the kingdom of heaven. This Spirit derived from heaven, is the birth of the Son of God, given to the soul as its savior, regenerator, or beginner of its return to heaven; it is that Word of life, or bruiser of the serpent, that was inspoken into the first fallen father of men; 'tis this alone that gives to all the race of Adam their capacity for salvation, their power of being again sons of God; and therefore, faith and prayer in the Name of Jesus Christ, or works done in the Spirit and power of Jesus Christ can alone save the soul, because the soul can have no relation to heaven, no communion with it, no beginning or power of growth in the heavenly life, but solely by the nature and Name of Jesus Christ derived into it. God's redemption of mankind is as universal as the fall: it was the one father of all men that fell, therefore, all his children were born into his fallen state: it was the one father of all men that was redeemed by the inspoken Word of life into him; therefore, all his children are born into his state of redemption, and have as certainly the same bruiser of the serpent in the birth of their life from him, as they have from him a serpentine nature that is to be bruised.

[App-1-141] Hence it was, that this bruiser of the serpent, when born of a virgin, and come to die for the world, saith of himself,"I am the way, the truth, and the life; no man cometh unto the Father but by me." Hence also the apostle saith, "There is no other name under heaven given among men, whereby we must be saved," because he is that same saving Name, or power of salvation which from the beginning was given to Adam, as an inspoken Word of life, or bruiser of the serpent: and therefore, as sure as Adam had any power of salvation derived into him from Jesus Christ, so sure was it, that the apostle must tell both Jews and heathens, that there was no salvation in any other.

[App-1-142] Therefore, though Jesus Christ is the one only savior of all that can anywhere, or at any time be saved, yet there is no partiality in God, because, this same Jesus Christ, who came in human flesh to the Jews in a certain age, was that same savior who was given to Adam, when all mankind were in his loins; and who, through all ages, and in all countries, from the first patriarchs to the end of the world, is the common savior, as he is the common light that lighteth every man that cometh into the world, and that principle of life both in Jews and heathens, by which they had any relation to God, or any power, or right, or ability to call him Father. When therefore you look upon the gospel as narrowing the way of salvation, or limiting it to those, who only know and believe in Jesus Christ, since his appearance in the flesh, you mistake the whole nature of the Christian redemption.

[App-1-143] And when you reject this savior that then appeared, and died as a sacrifice upon the cross, you don't renounce a particular kind of religion, that was given only at a certain time to one part of the world, but you renounce the one source and foundation of all the grace and mercy that God can bestow upon mankind, you renounce your share of that first covenant which God made with all men in Adam, you go back into his first fallen state, and so put yourself into that condition of eternal death, from which there is no possibility of deliverance, but by that one savior whom you have renounced.

[App-1-144] And now, my dear friend, beware of prejudice, or hardness of heart: one careless, or one relenting thought upon all that is here laid before you, may either quite shut out, or quite open an entrance for true conviction. I have shown you what is meant by Christian redemption, and the absolute necessity of a new and heavenly birth, in order to obtain your share of a heavenly life in the next world: I have confirmed the truths of the gospel, by proofs taken from what is undeniable in nature: and I readily grant you that nothing can be true in revealed religion, but what has its foundation in nature; because a religion coming from the God of nature, can have no other end but to reform, and set right the failings, transgressions, and violations of nature. When the gospel saith that man fallen from the state of his creation, and become an earthly animal of this temporal world, must be born again of the Son and Holy Spirit of God, in order to be a heavenly creature; 'tis because all nature saith, that an immortal, eternal soul, must have an immortal, eternal Light and Spirit, to make it live in eternal nature, as every animal must have a temporal light and spirit, in order to live in temporary nature. Must you not therefore either deny the immortality of the soul, or acknowledge the necessity of its having an eternal Light and Spirit? When the gospel saith, that nothing can kindle or generate the heavenly life, but the operation of the Light and Spirit of heaven, it is because all nature saith, that no temporal life can be raised but in the same manner in temporary nature. Must you not therefore be forced to confess, that nature and the gospel both preach the same truths.

[App-1-145] Light and spirit must be wherever there are living beings: and there must be the same difference betwixt the light and spirit of different worlds, as there is betwixt the worlds themselves. Hell must have its light, or it could have no living inhabitants, but its light is not so refreshing, not so gentle, not so lightful, not so comfortable as flashing points of fire in the thickest darkness of night; and therefore their light is called an eternal darkness, because it can never disperse, but only horribly discover darkness: hell also must have its spirit; but it is only an incessant insensibility of wrathful agitations, of which the thunder and rage of a tempest is but a low, shadowy resemblance, as being only a little outward eruption of that wrath, which is the inward, restless essence of the spirit of hell; and therefore that life, though it be a living spirit, is justly called an eternal death.

[App-1-146] The Light and Spirit of God admit of no delineation or comparison, they are only so far known to anyone, as they are brought into the soul by a birth of themselves in it.

[App-1-147] Now consider, I pray you: the light and spirit of this world can no more be the light and spirit of immortal souls, than grass and hay can be the food of angels; but is as different from the Light and Spirit of heaven, as an angel is different from a beast of the field. When therefore the soul of a man departs from his body, and is eternally cut off from all temporal light and spirit, what is it that can keep such a soul from falling into eternal darkness, unless it have in itself, that Light and Spirit, which is of the same nature with the Light and Spirit of eternity, so that it may be in the light of heaven or eternal nature, as it was in the light of this world in temporary nature.

[App-1-148] Light and spirit there must be in everything that lives, but the death of the body takes away the light and spirit of this world; if therefore the Light and Spirit of heaven be not born in the soul when it loses the body, it can only have that light and spirit, which is the very death and darkness of hell.

[App-1-149] When man lost the Light and Spirit of his creation, he lost it by turning the will and desire of his soul into an earthly life; this was his desire of knowing good and evil in this world. His fall therefore consisted in this, his soul lost its first innate, inbreathed Light and Spirit of heaven, and instead of it, had only the light and spirit of temporary nature, to keep up for a time such a life in him from this world, as the proper creatures of this world have: and this is the reason, why man, the noblest creature that is in this world, has yet various circumstances of necessity, poverty, distress and shame, that are not common to other animals of this world. 'Tis because the creatures of this life are here at home, are the proper inhabitants of this world, and therefore that womb out of which they are born, has provided them with all that they want; but man being only fallen into it, and as a transgressor, must in many respects find himself in such wants as other creatures have not. Transitory time has brought them forth, and therefore they can have no pain, nor concern, nor danger in passing away; because it is the very form of their nature, to begin, and to have an end: and therefore the God of nature has no outward laws, or directions for the creatures of this world.

[App-1-150] But the soul of man being not born of the light and spirit of this transitory world, but only standing a while as a stranger upon earth, and being under a necessity of having either the nature of an angel, or a devil, when it leaves this world, is met by the mercy and goodness of the God of nature, is inwardly and outwardly called, warned, directed, and assisted how to regain that Light and Spirit of heaven which it lost, when it fell under the temporary light and spirit of this world. And this is the whole ground and end of revealed religion, viz., to kindle such a beginning or birth of the divine Light and Spirit in the soul, that when man must take an eternal leave of the light and spirit of this world, he may not be in a state of eternal death and darkness.

[App-1-151] Now, seeing the Light and Spirit of heaven or eternal nature, is as different from the light and spirit of this world, as an angel is from an animal of the field, if you have lived here only to the spirit and temper of this world, governed by its goods and evils, and only wise according to its wisdom, you must die as destitute of the Light and Spirit of heaven, as the beasts that perish. You have now an aversion and dislike, or at least, a disbelief of the doctrines of Christian regeneration, you struggle against this kind of redemption, you would have no salvation from the Light and Spirit of eternity regenerated in your soul; where then must you be, when the light and spirit of this world leaves you?

[App-1-152] Do you think that the Light and Spirit of God will then seize upon you, shine up in you by an outward force, though they never could be born in you? Or do you think, that the Light and Spirit of God can now be generating themselves in you, and ready to appear, as soon as you have ended a life, that has continually resisted them, and would have no new birth from them? Or that God, by a compassionate goodness, will not suffer you to be in that condition, into which your own will has brought you? No, my friend, the will that is in you, must do that for you, which the will that was in angels did for those that stood, and for those that fell.

[App-1-153] God's goodness or compassion is always in the same infinite state, always flowing forth, in and through all nature in the same infinite manner, and nothing wants it, but that which cannot receive it: whilst the angels stood, they stood encompassed with the infinite source of all goodness and compassion, God was communicated to them in as high a degree as their nature could receive; and they fell, not because he ceased to be an infinite, open fountain of all good to them, but because they had a will which must direct itself.

[App-1-154] For the will, at its first arising in the creature, can be subject to no outward power, because it has no outward maker; as it stands in a creaturely form, God is its true creator; but as a will, it has no outward maker, but is a ray, or spark, derived from the unbeginning will of the creator, and is of the same nature in the creature, as it was in the creator, self-existent, self-generating, self -moving, and uncontrollable from without; and there could not possibly be a free will in the creature, but by its being directly derived, or propagated from the same will in the creator, for nothing can be free now, but that which always was so.

[App-1-155] But if the free will of God, which is above and superior to nature, be communicated to the creature, then the creature's free will must have the same power over its one nature, that the will of God has over that eternal nature, which is his own manifestation: and therefore, every free creature must have, and find its own nature in this, or that state, as a birth from the free working of its own will. And here appears the true reason, why no creatures of this world can commit sin; 'tis because they have no will that is superior to nature: their will in every one of them, is only the will of nature; and therefore let them do what they will, they are always doing that which is natural, and consequently, not sinful. But the will of angels and men being an offspring, or ray, derived from the will of God, which is superior to nature, stands chargeable with the state and condition of their nature; and therefore it is, that the nature of the devil, and the nature of fallen man is imputed to both of them, as their sin, which could not be, but because their will was uncontrollable, and gave birth and being to that state and condition of nature, which is called, and is their sin.

[App-1-156] Therefore, O man! look well to thyself, and see what birth thou art bringing forth, what nature is growing up in thee, and be assured, that stand thou must, in that state of nature, which the working of thy own will has brought forth in thee, whether it be happy or miserable. Expect no arbitrary goodness, of God towards thee, when thou leavest this world; for that must grow for ever which hath grown here. God hath created thee in nature, his mercy hath shown thee all the laws and necessities of nature, his mercy hath shown thee all the laws and necessities of nature, and how thou mayest rise from thy corruption, according to the possibilities of nature, and he can only save thee by thy conforming to the demands of nature: the greatness of the divine mercy and favor towards all men appears in this, that when all nature had failed, and mankind could from nature have nothing but eternal death, that God brought such a second Adam into the world, as being God and man, could make nature begin its work again, where it failed in the first Adam.

[App-1-157] The free grace and mercy by which we are said in the scripture to be saved, is not an arbitrary good will in God, which saves whom he pleases; as a prince may forgive some, and not forgive others, merely through his own sovereign grace and favor: nothing of this kind hath any place in God, or in the mystery of our redemption; but the mercy and grace, by which we are saved, is therefore free, because God hath freely, and from his own goodness, put us into a state and possibility of salvation, by freely giving us Jesus Christ, (the divine and human nature united in one person) as the only means of regenerating that first divine and human life, which the whole race of mankind had lost. In this sense alone it is, that all our salvation is wholly owing to the free grace of God, that is, our state, and possibility, and means of attaining salvation is wholly owing to his free grace in giving us Jesus Christ; but our salvation, considered as a finished thing, is not, cannot be found by any act of God's free grace towards us, but because all that is done, altered, removed, suppressed, quickened, and recovered by us in the state of our nature, which the free grace of God had furnished us with the possibility and means of doing. If nature and creature had no share in working out our salvation; if it was all free grace, effected against, and without the powers of nature, how comes it, that the fallen angels are not to be redeemed as well as man? Must we say that God is less good to them than he is to us? Or if they are not redeemed, can there be any other reason for it, but because it is an impossibility in nature? Must not an infinite good do all the good that is wanted, and is possible to be done? If free grace can do what it pleases, if it wants no concurrence of nature and creature, how can any being, whether man or angel, be eternally miserable, but through an eternal defect in the goodness of God towards it? Shall we call that infinite goodness, which sets bounds and limits to itself, and which could do more good, but will not?

[App-1-158] The truth of the matter is this, God is as infinite and boundless in love and goodness, as he is in power, but his omnipotence can only do that which is possible, and nothing is possible but that which hath its possibility in nature; because nature is God's first power, his great, universal manifestation of his Deity, in and through, and by which all his infinite attributes break forth, and display themselves: so that to expect, that God should do anything that is above, or contrary to this nature, is as absurd as to expect that God should act above, or contrary to himself: as God can only make a creature to be in, and through, and by nature; so the reason why he cannot make a creature to be, and not to be at the same time, is only this, because it is contrary to nature. Let no man therefore trust to be saved at the last day, by any arbitrary goodness, or free grace of God; for salvation is, and can be nothing else, but the having put off all that is damnable and hellish in our nature, which salvation can be found by no creature but by its own full conforming to, and concurring with those mysterious means, which the free grace of God hath afforded for the recovery of our first, perfect, glorious state in nature.

Chapter II

Of Eternal and Temporal Nature. How Nature is from God, and the Scene of his Action. How the Creatures are out of it. Temporal Nature created out of that which is eternal. The fallen Angels brought the first Disorders into Nature. This World created to repair those Disorders. Whence Good and Evil is in every Thing of this World. How Heaven and Hell make up the Whole of this World. How the Fire of this World differs from eternal Fire; and the Matter of this World from the Materiality of Heaven. Eternal Nature is the Kingdom of Heaven, the beatific Manifestation of the triune God. God is more Love and Goodness. How Wrath and Anger come to be ascribed to him. Of Fire in general. Of the Unbeginning Fire. Of the Spirituality of Fire. How Fire comes to be in material Things. Whence the Possibility of kindling Fire in the Things of this World. Every Man is, and must be the Kindler of his own Eternal Fire, &c.

[App-2-1] Was there no nature, there could be no creature, because the life of every creature is, and can be nothing else, but the life of that nature out of which it was created, and in which it has its being. Eternal beings must have their qualities, nature, form and manner of existence out of eternal nature, and temporal beings out of temporary nature: was there no eternity, there could be no time, was there nothing infinite, there could be nothing finite; therefore we have here two great fundamental truths that cannot be shaken; first, that there is, and must be, an eternal nature; because there is a nature that is temporary, and that it must be that to eternal creatures, which temporal nature is to temporal creatures: secondly, that everywhere, and in all worlds, nature must stand between God and the creature, as the foundation of all mutual intercourse; God can transact nothing with the creature, nor the creature have any communion with God, but in, and by that nature, in which it stands.

[App-2-2] I hope no one will here ask me for scripture proofs of this, or call these truths nostrums, because they are not to be found in the same form of expression in some particular text of scripture. Where do the holy writings tell us, that a thing cannot be, and not be at the same time? Or that every consequence must arise from premises? And yet the scripture is continually supposing both these truths, and there could be no truth in the scripture, or anywhere else, if these things were not undeniable.

[App-2-3] There is nothing said of man throughout all scripture, but what supposes him to stand in nature, under a necessity of choosing something that is natural, either life or death, fire or water. There is nothing said of God with relation to creatures, but what supposes him to be the God of nature, manifesting himself in and through nature, calling, assisting and directing everything to its highest natural state. Nature is the scene of his providence, and all the variety of his governing attributes display themselves by his various operations in and through nature: therefore it is equally certain, that what God does to any creature, must be done through the medium of nature, and also what the creature does toward God, must be done in and through the powers of that nature in which it stands. No temporary creature can turn to God, or reach after him, or have any communication with him, but in, and according to that relation which temporary nature bears to God; nor can any eternal beings draw near to, or unite with God in any other manner, than that in which eternal nature is united with him. Would you know, why no omnipotence of God can create temporal animals but out of temporary nature, nor eternal animals but out of eternal nature; it is because no omnipotence of God can produce a visible triangle, but out of, and by three visible lines; for, as lines must be before there can be any lineal figures, so nature must be before there can be natural creatures.

[App-2-4] 2. Everything that is in being, is either God, or nature, or creature; and everything that is not God, is only a manifestation of God; for as there is nothing, neither nature, nor creature, but what must have its being in, and from God, so everything is, and must be according to its nature, more or less a manifestation of God. Everything therefore, by its form and condition, speaks so much of God, and God in everything, speaks and manifests so much of himself. Temporary nature is this beginning, created system of sun, stars, and elements; 'tis temporary nature, because it begins and hath an end, and therefore is only a temporary manifestation of God, or God manifested according to transitory things.

[App-2-5] 3. Properly and strictly speaking, nothing can begin to be: the beginning of everything is nothing more, than its beginning to be in a new state. Thus time itself does not begin to be, but duration, which always was, began to be measured by the earth's turning round, or the rising and setting of the sun, and that is called the beginning of time, which is, properly speaking, only the beginning of the measure of duration: thus it is with all temporal nature, and all the qualities and powers of temporal beings that live in it: no quality or power of nature then began to be, but such qualities and powers as had been from all eternity, began then to be in a new state. Ask what time is, it is nothing else but something of eternal duration become finite, measurable, and transitory? Ask what fire, light, darkness, air, water, and earth are; they are, and can be nothing else, but some eternal things become gross, finite, measurable, divisible, and transitory? For if there could be a temporal fire that did not spring out of eternal fire, then there might be time that did not come out of eternity.

[App-2-6] 'Tis thus with every temporary thing, and the qualities of it; 'tis the beginning of nothing, but only of a new state of something that existed before: therefore all temporary nature is a product, offspring, or outbirth of eternal nature, and is nothing else but so much of eternal nature changed from its eternal to a temporal condition. Fire did not begin to be, darkness did not begin to be, light did not begin to be, water and earth did not begin to be, when this temporary world first appeared, but all these things came out of their eternal state, into a lower, divided, compacted, created and transitory state. Hearing, seeing, tasting, smelling, feeling, did not then begin to be, when God first created the creatures of this world, they only came to be qualities and powers of a lower, and more imperfect order of beings than they had been before.

[App-2-7] Figures, and their relations, did not then begin to be, when material circles and squares, &c., were first made, but these figures and relations began then to appear in a lower state than they had done before: and so it must be said of all temporal nature, and everything in it. It is only something of eternal nature separated, changed, or created into a new, temporary state and condition.

[App-2-8] 4. Now it may be asked, why was eternal nature thus degraded, debased, and changed from its eternal state of perfection? Will anyone say, that God of his own free will changed eternal nature, which is the glorious manifestation of his power and godhead, the seat of his holy residence, his majestic kingdom of heaven, into this poor, miserable mixture of good and evil, into this impure state of division, grossness, death, and darkness? No. It is the highest of all absurdities, to say so. Now, we sufficiently know from scripture, that a whole hierarchy, or host of angels, renounced their heavenly life, and thereby raised up a kingdom that was not heavenly. Could they not have inflamed and disordered outward nature in which they lived, they could not have destroyed the heavenly nature in themselves: for everything must be according to the state of that world in which it lives; and therefore, the state of outward nature, and the state of inward nature in the angels must stand and fall together; and as sure as a whole kingdom of angels lost their heavenly life, so sure it is, that their whole kingdom lost its heavenly state and condition: and therefore, it is an undeniable truth, founded on scripture evidence, that same part of eternal nature was changed from its first state of glory and perfection, before the creation of temporary nature; therefore, in the creation of this poor, gross, disordered, perishable, material world, one of these two things was done, either God took the spoiled part of heaven or eternal nature, and created it into this temporary state of good and evil; or he degraded, and brought down some part of the kingdom of heaven from its glory and perfection, into this mixture of good and evil, order and disorder in which the world stands. He could not do this latter, without bringing evil into nature, as the devil had done, and therefore we may be sure he did not do it; but if he did the former, then the creation of this lower world, was a glorious act, and worthy of the infinite goodness of God, it was putting an end to the devil's working evil in nature, and it was putting the evil that was brought into nature, in a way of being finally overcome, and turned into good again. Will anyone now call these things whimsical speculations? Can anything be thought of more worthy of God, more conformable to nature, or more consonant to all revealed religion? But perhaps you will say, how could the angels spoil or destroy that glorious kingdom of eternal nature in which they dwelt. It may be answered, how could it possibly be otherwise? How could they live in eternal nature, unless nature without them, and nature within them, mutually mixed and qualified with each other? Would you have such mighty spirits, with their eternal energies, have less power in that nature, or kingdom in which they dwelt, than a kindled piece of coal hath in this world? For every piece of coal set on fire, adds so much heat to outward nature, and so far alters and changes the state of it.

[App-2-9] 5. Now, let it be supposed, not only that a piece of coal, but that the whole of everything in this world, that could either give or receive fire was made to burn, what effect would it have upon the whole frame of nature? Would not the whole state of things, the regions, places, and divisions of the elements, and all the order of temporal nature be quite destroyed?

[App-2-10] When therefore every angelical life kindled itself in wrath, and became thereby divided, darkened, and separated from God, the same kindling, darkening, dividing, and confusion must be brought forth in their natural kingdom, because they lived in nature, and could have neither love, nor wrath, but such as they could exert in and by the powers of nature.

[App-2-11] Now, all fire, wherever it is, is either a fire of wrath, or a fire of love: fire not overcome or governed by light, is the fire of wrath, which only tears in pieces, consumes and devours all that it can lay hold of, and it wills nothing else: but light is the fire of love, it is meek, amiable, full of kind embraces, lovingly spreading itself, and giving itself with all its riches into everything that can receive it. These are the two fires of eternal nature, which were but one in heaven, and can be only one wherever heaven is; and it was the separation of these two fires that changed the angels into devils, and made their kingdom a beginning of hell.

[App-2-12] Now, either of these two fires, wherever it is kindled in animate or lifeless things, communicates its own kind of heat in some degree to outward nature, and so far alters and changes the state of it: the wrath of a man, and the wrath of a tempest do one and the same thing to outward nature, alter its state in the same manner, and only differ in their degree of doing it.

[App-2-13] Fire kindled in a material thing, can only communicate with the materiality of nature; but the fire of a wrathfully-inflamed man, being a fire both of body and soul, communicates a twofold heat, it stirs up the fire of outward nature, as fire does in a coal, and it stirs up the wrath of hell as the devils do.

[App-2-14] The fire of love kindled by the Light and Spirit of God in a truly regenerated man, communicates a twofold blessing, it outwardly joins with the meek light of the sun, and helps to overcome the wrath of outward nature; it inwardly cooperates with the power of good angels, in resisting the wrath and darkness of hell: and it would be no folly to suppose, that if all human breath was become a mere, unmixed wrath, that all the fire in outward nature would immediately break forth, and bring that dissolution upon outward nature, which will arise from the last fire. Therefore it is necessary, that a whole kingdom of angels should kindle the same wrath and disorder in outward nature that was in themselves; for being in eternal nature, and communicating with it, as temporal beings do in temporal nature, what they did in themselves, must be done in that nature or kingdom in which they lived, and moved, and had their being.

[App-2-15] What a powerful fire there is in the wrath of a spirit, may be seen by the effects of human wrath; one sudden thought shall in a moment discolor, poison, inflame, swell, distort and agitate the whole body of a man. Whence also is it, that a diseased body infects the air, or that malignant air infects a healthful body? Is it not because there is, and must be an inseparable qualifying, mixing and uniting betwixt nature and those creatures that live in it? Now, all diseases and malignities, whether in nature or creature, all proceed from the sinful motions of the will and desires of the creature. This is as certain, as that death and all that leads to it, is the sole product of sin; therefore it is a certain truth, that all the disorder that ever was, or can be in nature, arises from that power which the creature hath in and upon nature; and therefore, as sure as a whole host of heavenly beings, raised up a fiery, wrathful, dark nature in themselves, so sure is it, that the same wrathful, fiery, dark disorder was raised up in that kingdom, or nature, in which they had their being.

[App-2-16] 6. Now the scriptures nowhere say in express words, that the place of this world was the place of the angels that fell, and that their fallen, spoiled and disordered kingdom, was by the power of God, changed or created into this temporary state of things in which we live; this is not expressly said, because it is plainly implied and fully signified to us by the most general doctrines of scripture; for if we know, both from nature and scripture, that this world is a mixture of good and evil, do not we enough know, that it could only be created out of that which was good and evil? And if we know that evil cannot come from God, if we know that the devil had actually brought it forth before the creation of this world; are we not enough told, that the evil which is in this world, is the evil that was brought forth into nature by the devil? And that therefore the matter of this world, is that very materiality which was spoiled by the fallen angels? How can we need a particular text of scripture to tell us, that the place of this world was the place of the angels before their fall, when the whole tenor of scripture tells us, that it is the place of their habitation now? For how could they have, or find darkness, but in that very place, where they had extinguished the light? What could they have to do with us, or we with them, but that we are entered into their possessions, and have their kingdom made over to us? How could they go about amongst us as roaring lions, seeking whom they may devour, but that our creation has brought us amongst them? They cannot possibly be anywhere, but where they fell, because they can live nowhere but in the evil which they have brought forth; they can have no wrath and darkness but where they broke off from light and love; they can communicate with no outward nature but that which fell with them, and underwent the same change as they did: therefore, though St. Jude saith with great truth, that they left their own habitations, yet, it is only as they left their own angelical nature, not departed from it into a distant place, but deformed and changed it; so that the heaven that was within them, and without them, is equally left, because both within them, and without them, they have no habitation but a fiery darkness broken off from the light of God.

[App-2-17] And therefore, as man by his creation is brought into a power of commerce with those fallen angels, who must live, and could only act in that part of nature which they had deformed, it is plain, that this creation placed him in that system of things, which was formed and created out of their fallen kingdom, because they can act, or be acted upon nowhere else.

[App-2-18] 7. And this is the one true, and only reason, why there is good and evil throughout all temporal nature and creature; 'tis because all this temporary nature is a creation out of that strife of evil against good which the fallen angels had brought into their kingdom. No subtle, evil serpent could have been generated, no tree of knowledge of good and evil could have been sprung out of the earth, but because nature in this world was that part of eternal nature which the fallen angels had corrupted; and therefore, a life made up of good and evil could be brought forth by it. Evil and good was in the angelical kingdom as soon as they set their wills and desires contrary to God, and the divine life. Had God permitted them to go on, their whole kingdom had been like themselves, all over one unmixed evil, and so had been incapable of being created into a redeemable state: but God put a stop to the progress of evil in their kingdom, he came upon it whilst it was in strife, and compacted or created it all into a new, temporary, material state and condition; whence these two things followed: first, that the fallen angels lost their power over it, and could no further kindle their own fire in it, but were as chained prisoners, in an extent of darkness which they could neither get out of, nor extend any further: secondly, this new creation being created out of this begun strife, stood as yet in the birth of life, and so became capable of being assisted and blessed by God; and finally, at the end of time, restored to its first heavenly state.

[App-2-19] Now, the good and evil that is in this world is that same good and evil, and in the same strife that it was in the kingdom of fallen angels, only with this happy difference, there it was under the devil's power, and in a way to be wholly evil; here it is in a new compacted, or created state under the providence and blessing of God, appointed to bring forth a new kind of life, and display the wonders of divine love, till such time as a new race of angelical creatures born in this mixture of good and evil, shall be fit to receive the kingdom of Lucifer, restored to its first glory?

[App-2-20] Is there any part of the Christian religion that does not either suppose or speak this great truth, any part of outward nature that does not confirm it? Is there any part of the Christian religion that is not made more intelligible, more beautiful and edifying by it? Is there any difficulty of outward nature that is not totally removed and satisfied by it?

[App-2-21] How was the philosophy of the ancient sages perplexed with the state of nature? They knew God to be all goodness, love, and perfection, and so knew not what to do with the misery of human life, and the disorders of outward nature, because they knew not how this nature came into its present state, or from whence it was descended. But had they known, that temporal nature, all that we see in this whole frame of things, was only the sickly, defiled state of eternal things put into a temporary state of recovery, that time and all transitory things were only in this war and strife, to be finally delivered from all the evil that was brought into eternal nature, their hearts must have praised God for this creation of things as those morning stars did, that shouted for joy when it was first brought forth.

[App-2-22] 8. From this true knowledge of the state, and nature, and place of this creation, what a reasonableness, wisdom, and necessity does there appear in the hardest sayings, precepts and doctrines of the gospel? He that thus knows what this world is, has great reason to be glad that he is born into it, and yet still greater reason to rejoice, in being called out of it, preserved from it, and shown how to escape with the preservation of his soul. The evils that are in this world, are the evils of hell, that are tending to be nothing else but hell; they are the remains of the sin and poison of the fallen angels: the good that is in this world are the sparks of life that are to generate heaven, and gain the restoration of the first kingdom of Lucifer. Who therefore would think of anything, desire anything, endeavor anything, but to resist evil in every kind, under every shape and color? Who would have any views, desires and prayers after anything, but that the life and light of heaven may rise up in himself, and that God's kingdom may come, and his will be done in all nature and creature?

[App-2-23] Darkness, light, fire and air, water and earth, stand in their temporary, created distinction and strife, for no other end, with no other view, but that they may obtain the one thing needful, their first condition in heaven: and shall man that is born into time for no other end, on no other errand, but that he may be an angel in eternity, think it hard to live as if there were but one thing needful for him? What was the poor politics, the earthly wisdom, the ease, sensuality, and advancements of this world for us, but such fruits as must be eaten in hell? To be swelled with pride, to be fattened with sensuality, to grow great through craft, and load ourselves with earthly goods, is only living the life of beasts, that we may die the death of devils. On the other hand, to go starved out of this world, rich in nothing but heavenly tempers and desires, is taking from time all that we came for, and all that can go with us into eternity.

[App-2-24] 9. But to return to the further consideration of nature. As all temporary nature is nothing else but eternal nature brought out of its kindled, disordered strife, into a created or compacted distinction of its several parts, so it is plain, that the whole of this world, in all its working powers, is nothing else but a mixture of heaven and hell. There cannot be the smallest thing, or the smallest quality of anything in this world, but what is a quality of heaven or hell, discovered under a temporal form: everything that is disagreeable to the taste, to the sight, to our hearing, smelling or feeling, has its root and ground, and cause, in and from hell, and is as surely in its degree the working or manifestation of hell in this world, as the most diabolical malice and wickedness is: the stink of weeds, of mire, of all poisonous, corrupted things, shrieks, horrible sounds, wrathful fire, rage of tempests, and thick darkness, are all of them things that had no possibility of existence, till the fallen angels disordered the state of their kingdom; therefore, everything that is disagreeable and horrible in this life, everything that can afflict and terrify our senses, all the kinds of natural and moral evil, are only so much of the nature, effects, and manifestations of hell: for hell and evil are only two words for one and the same thing: the extent of one is the extent of the other, and all that can be ascribed to the one, must be ascribed to the other. On the other hand, all that is sweet, delightful and amiable in this world, in the serenity of the air, the fineness of the seasons, the joy of light, the melody of sounds, the beauty of colors, the fragrancy of smells, the splendor of precious stones, is nothing else but heaven breaking through the veil of this world, manifesting itself in such a degree, and darting forth in such variety so much of its own nature. So that heaven and hell are not only as near you, as constantly showing and proving themselves to all your senses, as day and night, but night itself is nothing else but hell breaking forth in such a degree, and the day is nothing else but a certain opening of heaven, to save us from the darkness that arises from hell.

[App-2-25] O man! consider thyself, here thou standest in the earnest, perpetual strife of good and evil, all nature is continually at work to bring about the great redemption; the whole creation is travailing in pain, and laborious working, to be delivered from the vanity of time, and will thou be asleep? Everything thou hearest, or seest, says nothing, shows nothing to thee, but what either eternal light, or eternal darkness hath brought forth; for as day and night divide the whole of our time, so heaven and hell divide the whole of our thoughts, words and actions. Stir which way thou wilt, do, or design what thou wilt, thou must be an agent with the one or with the other. Thou canst not stand still, because thou livest in the perpetual workings of temporal and eternal nature; if thou workest not with the good, the evil that is in nature carries thee along with it: thou hast the height and depth of eternity in thee, and therefore be doing what thou wilt, either in the closet, the field, the shop, or the church, thou art sowing that which grows, and must be reaped in eternity. Nothing of thine can vanish away, but every thought, motion, and desire of thy heart, has its effect either in the height of heaven, or the depth of hell: and as time is upon the wing, to put an end to the strife of good and evil, and bring about the last great separation of all things into their eternal state, with such speed art thou making haste either to be wholly an angel, or wholly a devil: O! therefore awake, watch and pray, join with all thy force with that goodness of God, which has created time and all things in it, to have a happy end in eternity.

[App-2-26] 10. Temporal nature opened to us by the Spirit of God becomes a volume of holy instruction to us, and leads us into all the mysteries and secrets of eternity: for as everything in temporal nature is descended out of that which is eternal, and stands as a palpable, visible outbirth of it; so when we know how to separate the grossness, death, and darkness of time from it, we find what it is in its eternal state. Fire, and light, and air in this world are not only a true resemblance of the Holy Trinity in Unity, but are the Trinity itself in its most outward, lowest kind of existence or manifestation; for there could be no fire, fire could not generate light, air could not proceed from both, these three could not be thus united, and thus divided, but because they have their root and original in the Trinity of the Deity. Fire compacted, created, separated from light and air, is the elemental fire of this world: fire uncreated, uncompacted, unseparated from light and air, is the heavenly fire of eternity: fire kindled in any material thing is only fire breaking out of its created, compacted state; it is nothing else but the awakening the spiritual properties of that thing, which being thus stirred up, strive to get rid of that material creation under which they are imprisoned: thus every kindled fire, with all its rage and fierceness, tears and divides, scatters and consumes that materiality under which it is imprisoned; and were not these spiritual properties imprisoned in matter, no material thing could be made to burn. And this is another proof, that the materiality of this world is come out of a higher, and spiritual state, because every matter upon earth can be made to discover spiritual properties concealed in it, and is indeed a compaction of nothing else. Fire is not, cannot be a material thing, it only makes itself visible and sensible by the destruction of matter; matter is its death and imprisonment, and it comes to life but by being able to agitate, divide, shake off, and consume that matter which held it in death and bondage; so that every time you see a fire kindled, you see nature striving in a low degree to get rid of the grossness of this material creation, and to do that which can alone be done by the last fire, when all the inward, spiritual properties hid in everything, in rocks, and stones, and earth, in sun, and stars, and elements, shall by the last trumpet be awakened and called forth: and this is a certain truth, that fire could nowhere now be kindled in any material thing, but for this reason, because all material nature was created to be restored, and stands by divine appointment in a fitness and tendency to have its deliverance from this created state, by fire; so that every time you see a piece of matter dissolved by fire, you have a full proof, that all the materiality of this world is appointed to a dissolution by fire; and that then, (O glorious day!) sun and stars, and all the elements will be delivered from vanity, will be again that one eternal, harmonious, glorious thing which they were, before they were compacted into material distinctions and separations.

[App-2-27] 11. The elements of this world stand in great strife and contrariety, and yet in great desire of mixing and uniting with each other; and hence arises both the life and death of all temporal things; and hereby we plainly know that the elements of this world were once one undivided thing; for union can nowhere be desired, but where there has first been a separation; as sure therefore as the elements desire each other, so sure is it, that they have been parted from each other, and are only parts of some one thing that has been divided. When the elements come to such a degree of union, a life is produced; but because they have still a contrariety to each other, they soon destroy again that same life which they had built, and therefore every four-elementary life is short and transitory.

[App-2-28] Now, from this undeniable state of nature, we are told these following great truths: 1. That the four elements are only four parts of that, which before the creation of the world, was only a one element, or one undivided power of life. 2. That the mortality of this life is wholly and solely owing to the divided state of the elements. 3. That the true, immortal life of nature, is only there to be found, where the four elements are only one thing, mere unity and harmony; where fire and air, water and earth, have a much more glorious union than they have in diamonds and precious stones: for in the brightest diamonds the four elements still partake of their divided state, though to our eye they appear as only one glorious thing; but the beauty of the diamond is but a shadow, a low specimen of that glory which will shine through all nature, when fire and air, water and earth shall be again that one thing which they were, before the fall of angels and the creation of this world. 4. That the body of Adam (being formed for immortality) could not possibly have the nature, or be made out of the divided state of the elements. The letter of scripture absolutely demonstrates this; for if sickness, sorrow, pain, the trouble of heat and cold, all so many forerunners of death, can only be where the

elements are in division and contrariety; and if, according to scripture, these calamities did not, could not possibly touch Adam till he fell, then it is plain from scripture, that before his fall, the division and contrariety of the elements was not in him: and that was his paradisaical nature, in and by which he stood in a state of superiority over all the elements of this world. 5. That the body of Adam lost is one elementary glory and immortality, and then first became gross, dark, heavy flesh and blood, under the power of the four elements, when he lusted to eat, and actually did eat of that tree, which had its good and evil from the divided state of the elements. 6. Hence we also know, with the greatest certainty, the mystery of the resurrection of the body, that it consists wholly and solely in the reducing the four-elementary body of this world, to its first, one elementary state, and then everyone has that same body raised again that died, and all that Adam lost is restored. For if the body is mortal, and dies because it is become a body of the four elements, it can only be raised immortal, by having its four elements reduced again into one: and here lies the true sameness of the body that died, and that which rises again. But to proceed:

[App-2-29] 12. As all the four elements, by their desiring, and wanting to be united together, prove that they are only four grossly divided outbirths of that which before was only one heavenly, harmonious element, so every single element fully demonstrates the same thing; for every single element, though standing in its created contrariety to every other, has yet in its own divided state, all the four elements in itself: thus the air has everything in it that is in the earth, and the earth has in itself everything that is in fire, water and air, only in a different mixture and compaction; were it not so, had not every element in some degree the whole nature of them all, they could not possibly mix, and qualify with one another; and this may well pass for a demonstration, that that out of which the four elements are descended, was one harmonious union of them all, because every one of the four, has now, and must have in its undivided state, all the four in itself, though not in equality; for if the four must be together, though unequally lodged in every single element, it is plain, the four must have been one harmonious thing, before they were brought into four unequal separations: and therefore, as sure as there are four warring, disagreeing elements in time, so sure is it, that that which is now in this fourfold division, was and is in eternity, one, in an heavenly, harmonious union, keeping up an eternal, joyful, glorious life in eternal nature, as its four broken parts bring forth a poor, miserable, transitory life in temporal nature.

[App-2-30] 13. All matter in this world is only the materiality of heaven thus altered. The difference between matter in this world and matter in the other world, lies wholly and solely in this; in the one it is dead, in the other it is living materiality. It is dead materiality in this world, because it is gross, dark, hard, heavy, divisible, &c. It is in this state of death, because it is separated, or broken off from the eternal light, which is the true life, or the power of life in everything.

[App-2-31] In eternal nature or the kingdom of heaven, materiality stands in life and light; it is the light's glorious body, or that garment wherewith light is clothed, and therefore has all the properties of light in it, and only differs from light, as it is its brightness and beauty, as the holder and displayer of all its colors, powers and virtues. But the same materiality in this world, being created or compacted into a separation from fire united with light, is become the body of death and darkness, and is therefore gross, thick, dark, heavy, divisible, &c., for death is nothing else but the shutting up, or shutting out the united power of fire and light: this is the only death that ever did, or can happen to anything, whether earthly or heavenly. Therefore, every degree of hardness, sickness, stiffness, &c., is a degree of death; and herein consists the deadness of the materiality of this world. When it shall be raised to life, that is, when the united power of fire and light shall kindle itself through all temporal nature, then hardness, darkness, divisibility, &c., will be all extinguished together.

[App-2-32] That the deadness of the earth may, and certainly will be brought to life by the united power of fire and light, is sufficiently shown us by the nature and office of the sun. The sun is the united power of fire and light, and therefore the sun is the raiser of life out of the deadness of the earth; but because fire and light as united in the sun, is only the virtue of temporary fire and light, so it can only raise a short and fading, transitory life. But as sure as you see, that fire and light united in the sun, can change the deadness of the earth, into such a beautiful variety of a vegetable life, so sure are you, that this dark, gross earth, is in its state of death and darkness, only for this reason, because it is broken off from the united power of fire and light: for as sure as the outward operation of the fire and light of the sun can change the deadness of the earth into a degree of life, so sure is it, that the earth lies in its present deadness, because it is separated from its own eternal fire and light: and as sure as you see, that the fire and light of the sun can raise a temporal life out of the earth, so sure is it, that the united power of eternal fire and light can, and will turn all that is earthly, into its first state of life and beauty. For the sun of this world, as it is the union of temporal fire and light, has no power, but as it is the outward agent, or temporary representative of eternal fire and light, and therefore it can only do that in part, and imperfectly in time, which by the eternal fire and light will be wholly and perfectly done in eternity. And therefore every vegetable life, every beauty, power, and virtue which the sun calls forth out of the earth, tells us, with a divine certainty, that there will come a time, when all that is hid in the deadness, grossness, and darkness of the earth, will be again called up to a perfection of life and glory of beauty.

[App-2-33] 14. How has the philosophy of the schools been puzzled with the divisibility of matter! It is because human reason, the mistress of the schools, partakes of the deadness of the earth; and the soul of man must first have the light of eternal life rise up in him, before he can see or find out the truths of nature. Human reason knew nothing of the death of the matter, or the nature and reason of its temporary creation, and so thought death and divisibility to be essential to matter; but the light of God tells every man this infallible truth, that God made not death in anything, that he is a God of life, and therefore, everything that comes from him, comes into a state of life. Matter is thick, hard, heavy, divisible, and the like, only for a time, because it is compacted or created into thickness, hardness, and divisibility only for a time: these are only the properties of its temporal, created state, and therefore are no more essential to it than the hardness of ice is essential to water. Now, that the creation of the matter of this world is nothing else but a compaction, that all the elements are separated compactions of that which before was free from such a compaction, is plain from scripture. For we are told, that all the material things and elements of this world, are to have their created state and nature taken from them, by being dissolved or melted: but if this be a scripture truth, then it is equally true from scripture, that their creation was only a compaction; and a compaction of something that stood before according to its own nature, absolutely free from it. Mortality, corruptibility, and divisibility, are not essential properties, but temporary accidents, they are in things, as diseases and sickness are, and are as separable from them; and that is the true reason, why this mortal can put on immortality, this corruptible can put on incorruptibility, and this divisible put on indivisibility: for when the four elements shall be dissolved and loosed from their separate compaction from one another, when fire and air, water and earth, shall be a one much more glorious and harmonious thing than they are now in the brightest diamond, then the divisibility of this redeemed materiality will be more impossible to be conceived, than the distance between fire and water in a diamond.

[App-2-34] 15. The reason why all inanimate things of this world tend towards their utmost perfection in their kind, lieth wholly and solely in this ground; it is because the four elements of this world were once the one element of the kingdom of the fallen angels; and therefore, nature in this world is always laboring after its first perfection of life, or as the scripture speaks, the "whole creation travaileth in pain, and groaneth to be delivered from its present vanity": and therefore it is, that all vegetables and fruits naturally grasp after every kind and degree of perfection they can take in; endeavoring with all their power, after that first perfection of life which was before the fall of the angels. Every taste and color, and power and virtue, would be what it was before Lucifer kindled his dark, fiery, wrathful kingdom; but as this cannot be, so when every fruit and flower has worked itself as far towards a heavenly perfection as it can, it is forced to wither and rot, and become a witness to this truth, that neither flesh nor blood, nor fruit, nor flower, can reach the kingdom of God.

[App-2-35] 16. All the misery and imperfection that is in temporary nature, arises from the divided state of the elements: their division is that which brings all kinds and degrees of death and hell into this world, and yet their being in a certain degree in one another, and always endeavoring after their first union, is so much of the nature and perfection of heaven still in them. The death that is in this world, consists in the grossness, hardness and darkness of its materiality. The wrath that is in this world consists in the kindled division of its qualities, whence there arises a contrary motion and fermentation in all its parts, in which consists both the life and death of all its creatures. This death and this wrath is the nature of hell in this world, and is the manifestation of the disorders which the fallen angels have occasioned in nature. The heaven in this world began when God said, Let there be light, for so far as light is in anything, so much it has of heaven in it, and of the beginning of a heavenly life: this shows itself in all things of this world, chiefly in the life-giving power of the sun, in the sweetness and meekness of qualities and tempers, in the softness of sounds, the beauty of colors, the fragrancy of smells, and richness of tastes and the like; thus far as anything is tinctured with light, so far it shows its descent from heaven, and its partaking of something heavenly and paradisaical. Again, love or desire of union, is the other part of heaven that is visible in this world. In things without life, it is a senseless desire, a friendly mixing and uniting of their qualities, whereby they strive to be again in that first state of unity and harmony in which they existed, before they were kindled into division by Lucifer. In rational creatures, it is meekness, benevolence, kindness and friendship amongst one another: and thus far they have heaven and the Spirit of God in them, each in their sphere, being and doing that to one another, which the divine love is and does to all.

[App-2-36] Again, the reason why man is naturally taken with beautiful objects, why he admires and rejoices at the sight of lucid and transparent bodies, and the splendor of precious stones, why he is delighted with the beauty of his own person, and is fond of his features when adorned with fine colors, has this only true ground, 'tis because he was created in the greatest perfection of beauty, to live amongst all the beauties of a glorious paradise: and therefore man, though fallen, has this strong sensibility and reaching desire after all the beauties, that can be picked up in fallen nature. Had not this been his case, had not beauty, and light, and the glory of brightness been his first state by creation, he would now no more want the beauty of objects, than the ox wants to have his pasture enclosed with beautiful walls, and painted gates. Every vanity of fallen man shows our first dignity, and the vanity of our desires are so many proofs of the reality of that which we are fallen from. Man wants to see himself in riches, greatness and power, because human nature came first into the world in that state; and therefore, what he had in reality in paradise, that is he vainly seeking for, where he is only a poor prisoner in the valley and shadow of death.

[App-2-37] 17. All beings that are purely of this world, have their existence in and dependence upon temporal nature. God is no maker, creator or governor of any being or creature of this world, immediately, or by himself, but he creates, upholds and governs all things of this world, by, and through, and with temporal nature: as temporary nature is nothing else but eternal nature separated, divided, compacted, made visible and changeable for a time, so heaven is nothing else but the beatific visibility, the majestic preference {presence?} of the abysmal, unsearchable, triune God: 'tis that light with which the scripture saith, God is decked as with a garment, and by which he is manifested and made visible to heavenly eyes and beings; for Father, Son, and Holy Ghost, as they are the triune God, deeper than the kingdom of heaven or eternal nature, are invisible to all created eyes; but that beatific visibility and outward glory which is called the kingdom of heaven, is the manifestation of the Father, Son, and Holy Ghost, in, and by, and through the glorious union of eternal fire, and light, and spirit. In the kingdom of heaven, these are three and one, because their original, the Holy Trinity, is so, and we must call them by the names of fire, and light, and spirit; because all that we have of fire, and light, and spirit in this world, has its whole nature directly from them, and is indeed nothing else but the fire, and light, and spirit of eternity, brought into a separated, compacted, temporal state. So that to speak of a heavenly fire, has no more grossness and offense in it, than when we speak of a heavenly life, a heavenly light, or heavenly spirit; for if there is a heavenly light and spirit, there must of all necessity be a heavenly fire; and if these things were not in heaven in a glorious state of union, they never could have been here in this gross state of a temporal compaction and division: so that as sure as there are fire, and light, and air in this world, in a divided, compacted, imperfect state, in which consists the life of temporary nature and creatures, so sure is it, that fire, and light, and spirit are in the kingdom of heaven, united in one perfection of glory, in which consists the beatific visibility of God, the divine nature, as communicable to heavenly beings.

[App-2-38] 18. The kingdom of heaven stands in this threefold life, where three are one, because it is a manifestation of the Deity, which is three and one; the Father has his distinct manifestation in the fire, which is always generating the light; the Son has his distinct manifestation of the light, which is always generated from the fire; the Holy Ghost has his manifestation in the spirit, that always proceeds from both, and is always united with them.

[App-2-39] It is this eternal unbeginning Trinity in Unity of fire, light, and spirit, that constitutes eternal nature, the kingdom of heaven, the heavenly Jerusalem, the divine life, the beatific visibility, the majestic glory and presence of God. Through this kingdom of heaven, or eternal nature, is the invisible God, the incomprehensible Trinity eternally breaking forth, and manifesting itself in a boundless height and depth of blissful wonders, opening and displaying itself to all its creatures as in an infinite variation and endless multiplicity of its powers, beauties, joys and glories. So that all the inhabitants of heaven are for ever knowing, seeing, hearing, feeling, and variously enjoying all that is great, amiable, infinite and glorious in the divine nature.

[App-2-40] Nothing ascends, or comes into this kingdom of heaven, but that which descended, or came out of it, all its inhabitants must be innate guests, and born out of it.

[App-2-41] 19. God considered in himself, as distinct from this eternal nature, or kingdom of heaven, is not the immediate creator of any angels, spirits, or divine beings; but as he creates and governs all temporal beings in, and by, and out of temporal nature, so he creates and governs all spiritual and heavenly beings in, and by, and out of eternal nature: this is as absolutely true, as that no being can be temporal, but by partaking of temporal nature, nor any being eternal, but by partaking of the eternal, divine nature; and therefore, whatever God creates is not created immediately by himself, but in and by, and out of that nature, in which it is to live, and move, and have its being, temporal beings out of temporal nature, and eternal beings out of the heavenly kingdom of eternal nature: and hence it is, that all angels, and the souls of men are said to be born of God, sons of God, and partakers of the divine nature, because they are formed out of that eternal nature, which is the unbeginning majesty of God, the kingdom of heaven, or visible glory of the Deity. In this eternal nature, which is the majestic clothing, or glory of the triune God, manifested in the glorious unity of divine fire, light, and spirit, have all the created images of God, whether they be angels or men, their existence, union and communion with God; because

fire, and light, and spirit have the same union and birth in the creature, as in the creator: and hence it is, that they are so many various mirrors of the Deity, penetrated with the majesty of God, receiving and returning back communications of the life of God. Now, in this ground, that is, in this consideration of God, as manifesting his Holy Trinity through nature and creature, lieth the solid and true understanding of all that is so variously said of God, both in the Old and New Testament with relation to mankind, both as to their creation, fall, and redemption. God is to be considered throughout, as the God of nature, only manifesting himself to all his creatures in a variety of attributes in and by nature; creating, governing, blessing, punishing, and redeeming them according to the powers, workings, and possibilities of nature. Fire, light, and spirit in harmonious union, is the substantial glory, the beatific manifestation of the triune God, visible and communicable to creatures formed out of it. All intelligent, holy beings were by God formed and created out of, and for the enjoyment of this kingdom of glory, and had fire, and light, and spirit, as the triune glory of their created being: and herein consisted the infinite love, goodness and bounty of God to all his creatures: it was their being made creatures of this fire, light, and spirit, partakers of that same nature in which the Holy Trinity had stood from all eternity gloriously manifested. And thus they were creatures, subjects, and objects of the

divine love; they came into the nearest, highest relation to God; they stood in, and partook of his own manifested nature, so that the outward glory and majesty of the triune God, was the very form, and beauty, and brightness of their own created nature. Every creature which thankfully, joyfully, and absolutely gave itself up to this blessed union with God, became absolutely fixed in its first created glory, and incapable of knowing anything but love, and joy, and happiness in God to all eternity: thus in this state, all angels and men came first out of the hands of God. But seeing light proceeds from fire by a birth, and the spirit from both, and seeing the will must be the leader of the birth, Lucifer and Adam could both do as they did, Lucifer could will strong might and power, to be greater than the light of God made him, and so he brought forth a birth of might and power, that was only mighty wrath and darkness, a fire of nature broken off from its light. Adam could will the knowledge of temporal nature, and so he lost the Light and Spirit of heaven for the light and spirit of this world: and had man been left in this state of temporary nature, without a redeemer, he must, when the light of this world had left him, have found himself in the same absolute wrath and darkness of nature, which the fallen angels are in.

[App-2-42] 20. Now, after these two falls of two orders of creatures, the Deity itself came to have new and strange names, new and unheard of tempers and inclinations of wrath, fury, and vengeance ascribed to it. I call them new, because they began at the fall; I call them strange, because they were foreign to the Deity, and could not belong to God in himself: thus God is in the scriptures said to be a consuming fire. But to whom? To the fallen angels, and lost souls. But why, and how is he so to them? It is because those creatures have lost all that they had from God, but fire; and therefore God can only be found and manifested in them, as a consuming fire. Now, is it not justly said, that God, who is nothing but infinite love, is yet in such creatures only a consuming fire, and that though God be nothing but love, yet they are under the wrath and vengeance of God, because they have only that fire in them, which is broken off from the light and love of God, and so can know, or feel nothing of God, but his fire in them? As creatures they can have no life, but what they have in and from God; and therefore, that wrathful life which they have, is truly said to be a wrath of God upon them. And yet it is as strictly true, that there is no wrath in God himself, that he is not changed in his temper towards the creatures, that he does not cease to be one and the same infinite fountain of goodness, infinitely flowing forth in the riches of his love upon all and every life; but the creatures have changed their state in nature, and so the God of nature can only be manifested in and to them, according to their own state in nature: and this is the true ground of rightly understanding all that is said of the wrath and vengeance of God in and upon the creatures. It is only in such a sense as the curse or unhappiness of God may be said to be upon them, not because anything cursed, or unhappy can be in, or come from God, but because they have made that life which they must have in God, to be mere curse and unhappiness to them: for every creature that lives, must have its life in and from God, and therefore God must be in every creature; this is as true of devils, as of holy angels: but how is God in them? Why only as he is manifested in nature. Holy angels have the triune life of God in them, therefore God is in them all love, goodness, majesty and glory, and theirs is the

kingdom of heaven. Devils have nothing of this triune life left in them, but the fire of eternal nature broken off from all light and joy; and therefore the life that they can have in and from God, is only a life of wrath and darkness, and theirs is the kingdom of hell: and because this life is a strength of life which they must have in and from God, and which they cannot take out of his hands; therefore, is their cursed, miserable, wrathful life truly and justly said to be the curse, and wrath, and vengeance of God in and upon them, though God himself can no more have wrath and vengeance, than he can have mischief and malice in him: for this is a glorious, twofold truth, that from God considered as in himself, nothing can come from eternity to eternity, but infinite love, goodness, happiness, and glory; and also that infinite love, goodness, happiness and glory are, and will be for ever and ever flowing forth from him in the same boundless, universal, infinite manner; he is the same infinitely overflowing fountain of love, goodness and glory after, as before the fall of any creatures; his love, and the infinite workings of it can no more be lessened, than his power can be increased by any outward thing; no creature, or number of creatures can raise any anger in him, 'tis as impossible as to cast terror, or darkness, and pain into him, for nothing can come into God from the creature, nothing can be in him, but that which the Holy Trinity in Unity is in itself. All creatures are products of the infinite, triune love of God; nothing willed, and desired, and formed them, but infinite love, and they have all of them all the happiness, beauty and excellency that an infinitely powerful love can reach out to

them: the same infinite love continues still in its first creating goodness, willing, desiring, working, and doing nothing with regard to all creatures, but what it willed, did, and desired in the creation of them: this God over nature and creature, darts no more anger at angels when fallen, than he did in the creation of them: they are not in hell, because Father, Son, and Holy Ghost are angry at them, and so cast them into a punishment, which their wrath had contrived for them; but they are in wrath and darkness, because they have done to the light which infinitely flows forth from God, as that man does to the light of the sun, who puts out his own eyes: he is in darkness, not because the sun is darkened towards him, has less light for him, or has lost all inclination to enlighten him, but because he has put out that birth of light in himself, which alone made him capable of seeing in the light of the sun. It is thus with fallen angels, they have extinguished in themselves that birth of light and love, which was their only capacity for that happiness, which infinitely, and everywhere flows forth from God; and they no more have their punishment from God himself than the man who puts out his eyes, has his darkness from the sun itself.

[App-2-43] 21. God, considered in himself, as the holy, triune God, is not the immediate fountain and original of creatures; but God considered as manifesting himself in and through nature, is the creator, Father and producer of all things. The hidden Deity of Father, Son, and Holy Ghost, is from eternity to eternity, manifested, made visible, perceivable, sensible in the united glory of fire, light and spirit; this is the beatific presence, the glorious outbirth of the Holy Trinity; this is that eternal, universal nature, which brings God into all creatures, and all creatures into God, according to that degree and manner of life which they have in nature: for the life of creatures must stand in nature, and nature is nothing else but God made manifest, visible, and perceptible; and therefore the life of every creature, be it what it will, a life of joy or wrath, is only so much of God made manifest in it, and perceptible by it, and thus is God in some creatures only a God of wrath, and in others, only a God of glory and goodness.

[App-2-44] No creature can have life, or live, and move, and have its being in God, but by being formed out of, and living in this manifestation of nature. Thus far hell and heaven, angels and devils are equally in God, that is, they equally live, move, and have their being in that eternal nature, which is the eternal manifestation of God: the one have a life of glory, majesty, and love, and bliss, the other a life of horror, fire, wrath, misery, and darkness. Now, all this could not possibly be, there could be no room for this distinction between creatures standing in nature, the one could not possibly have a life of majestic bliss and glory, the other of fiery horror and darkness, but because the holy, triune God is manifested in the united glory and bliss of fire, light, and spirit. For the creatures could only divide that, which there was in nature to be divided, they could only divide that, which was united, and divisible; and therefore, as sure as heaven is a splendrous light of blissful majesty, as sure as hell is a place of fiery wrath and darkness, so sure is it from the scriptures, that eternal nature, which is from God, or a manifestation of God, is a nature of united fire, light, and spirit, otherwise, some creatures could not have the blissful glory of light, and others, a horrible, fiery darkness for their separate portions.

[App-2-45] All therefore that has been said of an eternal nature, or kingdom of heaven, consisting of united fire, light, and spirit, is not only to be looked upon as an opinion well grounded, and sufficiently discovered by the light of nature, but as a fundamental truth of revealed religion, fully established by all that is said in the scriptures both of heaven and hell. For if God was not manifested, visible, perceptible and communicable, in and by this united fire, and light, and spirit, how could there be a heaven of glorious majesty? If this fire of heaven could not be separated, or broken off from its heavenly light, how could there be a hell in nature? Or, how could those angels which lost the light of heaven, have thereby fallen into a state of hellish darkness, or fire? Is not all this the greatest of demonstrations, that the holy Triunity of God is, and must be manifested in nature, by the union of fire, light, and spirit? And is not this demonstration wholly taken from the very letter of the most plain doctrines of scripture?

[App-2-46] Hell and wrath could have no possibility of existence, but because the light and majesty, and glory of heaven, must of all necessity have its birth in and from the fire of nature. An angel could not have become a devil, but because the angelic light and glory had, and must have its birth in and from the fire of life. And thus as a devil was found, where angelic light and glory had its existence, so a hell was found, where heavenly glory was before; and as the devil is nothing but a fire-spirit broken off from its angelic light and glory, so hell is nothing but the fire of heaven separated from its first light and majesty.

[App-2-47] And here we have plainly found two worlds in eternity; not possible to be two, nor ever known to be two, but by such creatures, as have in their own natures, by their own self-motion, separated the fire of eternal nature from its eternal light, spirit and majesty. And this is also the beginning, or first opening of the wrath of God in the creature; which is, in other words, only the beginning, or first opening of pain and misery in the creature, or the origin of a hellish, tormenting state of life.

[App-2-48] 22. And here, in this dark wrathful fire of the fallen creature, do we truly find that wrath and anger and vengeance of God, that cleaves to sin, that must be quenched, atoned, and satisfied before the sinner can be reconciled to God; that is, before it can have again that triune life of God in it, which is its union with the Holy Trinity of God, or its regaining the kingdom of heaven in itself.

[App-2-49] Some have objected, that by thus considering the fallen soul, as a dark, wrathful fire-spirit, for this reason, because it has lost the birth of the Son and Holy Spirit of God in it, that this casts reproach upon God the Father, as having the nature of such a soul in him. But this is a groundless objection, for this state of the soul casts no more reproach upon the first, than upon the second and third persons of the holy Trinity. The fallen soul, that has lost the birth of the Son and Holy Spirit of God in it, cannot be said to have the nature of the Father left in it. This would be blasphemous nonsense, and is no way founded on this doctrine. But such a soul must be said to have a nature from the Father left in it, though a spoiled one, and this because the Father is the origin, fountain and creator of all kind of existence: hell, and the devils have their nature from him, because every kind of creature must have what it has of life and being from its creator; but hell and the devils have not therefore the nature of the Father in them. If it be asked what the Father is, as he is the first person in the sacred Trinity, the answer must be, that as such, he is the generator of the Son and Holy Spirit: this is the nature of the Father; where this generating is not, there is not the nature of the Father. Is it not therefore highly absurd to charge this doctrine with ascribing the nature of the Father to the fallen soul, which asserts the soul to be fallen, for this reason, because it has quite lost and extinguished all power and ability for the birth of the Son and Holy Spirit in it? How could it be more roundly affirmed, or more fully proved, that the fallen soul hath not the nature of the Father in it. But to proceed:

[App-2-50] The reader ought not to wonder, or be offended at the frequent mention of the word "fire," which is here used to denote the true nature, and state of the soul. For both nature and scripture speak continually the same language. For wherever there is mention of life, light, or love in the scriptures, there fire is necessarily supposed, as being that in which all life, and light, and love must necessarily arise; and therefore the scriptures speak as often of fire, as they do of life, and light, and love, because the one necessarily includes the other: for all life, whether it be vegetable, sensitive, animal, or intellectual, is only a kindled fire of life in such a variety of states; and every dead, insensitive thing is only so, because its fire is quenched, or shut up in a hard compaction. If therefore we will speak of the true ground of the fallen state of men and angels, we are not at liberty to think of it under any other idea, or speak of it in any other manner, than as the darkened fire of their life, or the fire of their life unable to kindle itself into light and love. Do not the scriptures strictly confine us to this idea of hell? So that it is not any particular philosophy, or affected singularity of expression, that makes me speak in this manner of the soul, but because all nature and scripture forces us to confess, that the root of all and every life stands, and must necessarily stand in the properties of fire.

[App-2-51] The holy scriptures also speak much of fire, in the ideas which they give us, both of the divine nature, and of created spirits, whether they be saved, or lost; the former as becoming flames of heavenly light and love, the latter as dark firebrands of hell. {Theologia fere supra omnes sacrosanctam ignis figuram probasse reperitur. Eam enim invenies non solum retas igneas fingere, sed etiam ignea animalia--quinetiam thronos igneos esse dicit, ipsosq; summos seraphim incensos esse ex ipso nomine declarat, eisq; ignis & proprietatem & actionem tribuit: semperatq; ubiq; igneam figuram probat. Ac igneam quidem formam significare arbitror coelestium naturarum maximam in Deo imitando similitudinem. Theologi summam, & forma carentam essentiam ignis specie multis locis describunt, quod ignis multas divinae, si dictu fas est, proprietatis, imagines ac species prae se ferat. Ignis enim, qui sensu percipitur, in omnibus & per omnia sine admixtione funditur, secerniturq; a rebus omnibus, lucetq; totus simul, &

abstrusus est, incognitusq; manet ipse per se--cohiberi, vinciq; non potest--quicquid ipsi proprius quoquo modo adhibeatur, sui particeps facit. Renovat omnia vitali calore, illustrat aperto lumine; teneri non potest, nec misceri. Dissipandi vim habet, commutari non potest, sursum fertur, celeritate magna praeditus est, sublimis est, nec humilitatem ullam ferre potest. Immobilis est, per se movetur, aliis motum affert; comprehendendi vim habet, ipse comprehendi non potest. Non eget altero: clam se amplificat: in materiis quae ipsius capaces sunt, magnitudinem suam declarat. Vim efficiendi habet, potens est: omnibus praesto est; nec videtur: attritu autem quasi inquisitione quadam connaturaliter repente apparet, rursuq; ita avolat ut comprehendi, & detineri nequeat: in omnibus sui communionibus minui non potest--multas etiam alias ignis proprietates invenire possumus, que propria sunt divinae actionis. S. Dionis. Arcop. de coelesti Hierarci, 56.}

[App-2-52] No description is, or can be given us either of heaven or hell, but where fire is necessarily signified to be the ground and foundation both of the one and of the other. Why do all languages, however distant, and different from one another, all speak of the coldness of death, the coldness of insensibility? Why do they all agree in speaking of the warmth of life, the heat of passions, the burnings of wrath, the flames of love? It is because it is the voice or dictate of universal nature, that fire is the root or seat of life, and that every variety of human tempers is only the various workings of the fire of life. It ought to be no reason why we should think grossly of fire, because it is seen in so many gross things of this world? For how is it seen in them? Why only as a destroyer, a consumer, and refiner of all grossness; as a kindler of life, and light out of death and darkness. So that in all the appearances of fire, even in earthly things, we have reason to look upon it as something of a heavenly, exalting, and glorious nature; as that which disperses death, darkness, and grossness, and raises up the power and glory of every life.

[App-2-53] If you ask what fire is in its first, true, and unbeginning state, not yet entered into any creature, it is the power and strength, the glory and majesty of eternal nature; it is that which generates, enriches, brightens, strengthens and displays the Light of heaven. It is that which makes the eternal light to be majestic, the eternal love to be flaming: for the strength and vivacity of fire, must be both the majesty of light, and the ardor of love. It is the glorious outbirth, the true representative of God the Father eternally generating his only Son, Light and Word.

[App-2-54] If you ask what fire is in its own spiritual nature, it is merely a desire, and has no other nature than that of a working desire, which is continually its own kindler. For every desire is nothing else, but its own striking up, or its own kindling itself into some kind and degree of fire. And hence it is that nature (though reduced to great ignorance of itself) has yet forced all nations and languages to speak of its own desires, as cool, warm, or burning, &c., because every desire is, so far as it goes, a kindled fire. And it is to be observed, that fire could have no existence or operation in material things, but because all the matter of this world has in it more or less of spiritual and heavenly properties compacted in it, which continually desire to be delivered from their material imprisonment. And the stirring up the desire of these spiritual properties, is the kindling of that heat, and glance, and light, in material things, which we call fire, and is nothing else but their gloriously breaking, and triumphantly dispersing that hard compaction in which they were imprisoned. And thus does every kindled fire, as a flash or transitory opening of heavenly glory, show us in little and daily, but true instances, the triumph of the last fire, when all that is spiritual and heavenly in this world, shall kindle and separate itself from that, which must be the death and darkness of hell.

[App-2-55] Now the reason, why there are spiritual properties in all the essential things of this world, is only this, it is because the matter of this world is the materiality of the kingdom of heaven, brought down into a created state of grossness, death, and imprisonment, by occasion of the sin of those angels, who first inhabited the place, or extent of this material world.

[App-2-56] Now these heavenly properties, which were brought into this created compaction, lie in a continual desire to return to their first state of glory; and this is the groaning of the whole creation to be delivered from vanity, which the apostle speaks of. And in this continual desire lieth the kindling, and all the possibility of kindling any fire in the things of this world. Quench this desire, and suppose there is nothing in the matter of this world that desires to be restored to its first glory, and then all the breaking forth of fire, light, brightness, and glance in the things of this world, is utterly quenched with it, and it would be the same impossibility to strike fire, as to strike sense and reason out of a flint.

[App-2-57] 24. But you will perhaps say, though this be a truth, yet it is more speculative than edifying, more fitted to entertain the curiosity, than to assist the devotion of Christians. But stay awhile, and you shall see it is a truth full of the most edifying instruction, and directly speaking to the heart.

[App-2-58] For if every desire is in itself, in its own essence, the kindling of fire, then we are taught this great practical lesson, that our own desire is the kindler of our own fire, the former and raiser of that life which leads us. What our desire kindles, that becomes the fire of our life, and fits us either for the majestic glories of the kingdom of God, or the dark horrors of hell: so that our desire is all, it does all, and governs all, and all that we have and are, must arise from it, and therefore it is, that the scripture saith, "Keep thy heart with all diligence, for out of it are the issues of life."

[App-2-59] We are apt to think that our imaginations and desires may be played with, that they rise and fall away as nothing, because they do not always bring forth outward and visible effects. But indeed they are the greatest reality we have, and are the true formers and raisers of all that is real and solid in us. All outward power that we exercise in the things about us, is but as a shadow in comparison of that inward power, that resides in our will, imagination, and desires; these communicate with eternity, and kindle a life which always reaches either heaven or hell. This strength of the inward man makes all that is the angel, and all that is the devil in us, and we are neither good nor bad, but according to the working of that which is spiritual and invisible in us. Now our desire is not only thus powerful and productive of real effects, but it is always alive, always working and creating in us, I say creating, for it has no less power, it perpetually generates either life or death in us: and here lies the ground of the great efficacy of prayer, which when it is the prayer of the heart, the prayer of faith, has a kindling and creating power, and forms and transforms the soul into everything that its desires reach after: it has the key to the kingdom of heaven, and unlocks all its treasures, it opens, extends, and moves that in us, which has its being and motion in and with the divine nature, and so brings us into a real union and communion with God.

[App-2-60] Long offices of prayer sounded only from the mouth, or impure hearts, may year after year be repeated to no advantage, they leave us to grow old in our own poor, weak state: these are only the poor prayers of heathens, who, as our Lord said, "think to be heard by their much speaking." But when the eternal springs of the purified heart are stirred, when they stretch after that God from whence they came; then it is, that what we ask, we receive, and what we seek, we find. Hence it is, that all those great things are by the scriptures attributed to faith, that to it all things are possible; that it heals the sick, saves the sinner, can remove mountains, and that all things are possible to him that believeth; 'tis because the working of will and desire is the first eternal source of all power, that from which everything is kindled into that degree of life in which it standeth; 'tis because will and desire in us are creaturely offsprings of that first will and desire which formed and governed all things; and therefore, when the creaturely power of our will, imagination and desire leaves off its working in vanity, and gives itself wholly unto God in a naked and implicit faith in the divine operation upon it, then it is, that it does nothing in vain, it rises out of time into eternity, is in union and communion with God, and so all things are possible to it. Thus is this doctrine so far from being vainly speculative, that it opens to us the ground, and shows us the necessity and excellency of the greatest duties of the gospel.

[App-2-61] 25. Now, as all desire throughout nature and creature is but one and the same thing, branching itself out into various kinds and degrees of existence and operation, so there is but one fire throughout all nature and creature, standing only in different states and conditions. The fire that is in the light of the sun, is the same fire that is in the darkness of the flint: that fire which is the life of our bodies, is the life of our souls; that which tears wood in pieces, is the same which upholds the beauteous forms of angels: it is the same fire that burns straw, that will at last melt the sun, the same fire that brightens a diamond, is darkened in a flint: it is the same fire that kindles life in an animal, that kindled it in angels: in an angel it is an eternal fire of an eternal life, in an animal it is the same fire brought into a temporary condition, and therefore can only kindle a life that is temporary: the same fire that is mere wrath in a devil, is the sweetness of flaming love in an angel; and the same fire which is the majestic glory of heaven, makes the horror of hell.

Chapter III

[Intro,App-3] The true Ground of all the Doctrines of the Gospel discovered. Why Adam could make no Atonement for his sins. Why, and how Jesus Christ alone could make this Atonement. Whence the Shedding of Blood for the Remission of Sins. What Wrath and Anger it is, that is quenched and atoned by the Blood of Christ. Of the last Sufferings of Christ. Why, and how we must eat the Flesh and drink the Blood of Jesus Christ.

[App-3-1] We have now, worthy reader, so far cleared the way, that we have nothing to do, but to rejoice in the most open illustration, and full proof of all the great doctrines of the gospel, and to see all the objections, which Deists, Arians, and Socinians have brought against the first articles of our faith, dashed to pieces: for as soon as we but begin to know, that the holy, triune Deity from eternity to eternity manifests itself in nature, by the triune birth of fire, light and spirit, and that all angels and men must have been created out of this nature; there is not a doctrine in scripture concerning the creation, fall, and redemption of man, but becomes the most plainly intelligible, and all the mysteries of our redemption are proved and confirmed to us, by all that is visible and perceptible in all nature and creature.

[App-3-2] Here we have the plain foundation of the whole economy of all religion from the beginning to the end of time, why the incarnation of the Son of God, who is the light of the world, must have before it the fiery dispensation of the Father delivered from Mount Sinai; and after it, the pouring out, or proceeding forth of the Holy Spirit upon all flesh; it is because the triune life of the fallen race must be restored according to the triune manifestation of the holy Deity in nature.

[App-3-3] Here we know what the love, and what the anger of God is, what heaven and hell, an angel and a devil, a lost and a redeemed soul are. The love, and goodness, and blessing of God known, found, and enjoyed by any creature, is nothing else but the Holy Trinity of God known, found, and enjoyed in the blissful, glorious, triune life of fire, light and spirit, where Father, Son, and Holy Ghost perpetually communicate their own nameless, numberless, boundless powers, riches and glories to the created image of their own nature. The hell in nature, and the hellish life in the creature, the wrath of God in nature and creature, is nothing else but the triune, holy life broken and destroyed in some order of creatures, it is only the fire of heaven separated from its heavenly Light and Spirit. This is that eternal anger, and wrath, and vengeance, that must be atoned, satisfied, and removed, that eternal fire that must be quenched, that eternal darkness that must be changed into light, or there is no possibility in nature, that the soul of fallen man should ever see the kingdom of God: and here all the doctrines of the Socinians are quite torn up by the roots. For in this ground appeareth the absolute necessity of the incarnation, life, sufferings, death, resurrection and ascension of the Son of God. Here lieth the full proof, that through all nature there could no redeemer of man be found, but only in the second person of the adorable Trinity become man. For as the Light and Spirit of eternal life, is the Light and Spirit of the Son and Holy Ghost manifested in heaven, so the Light of eternal life could never come again into the fallen soul, but from him alone, who is the Light of heaven. He must be again in the soul, as he was in it when it was first breathed forth from the Holy Trinity, he must be manifested in the soul, as he is in heaven, or it can never have the life of heaven in it.

[App-3-4] The Socinians therefore, or others, who think they pay a just deference to the wisdom and omnipotence of God, when they suppose there was no absolute necessity for the incarnation of the Son of God; but that God, if he had so pleased, could as well have saved man some other way, show as great ignorance both of God and nature, as if they should have said, that when God makes a blind man to see by opening or giving him eyes, there was no necessity in the thing itself, that sight should be given in that particular way, but that God, if he had so pleased, could have made him become a seeing man in this world without eyes, or light of this world.

[App-3-5] For if the Son of God is the Light of heaven, and man only wants to be redeemed, because he has lost the Light of heaven; is it not absolutely impossible for him to be redeemed any other way, or by any other thing, than by a birth of this Son of God in him. Is not this particularity the one only thing that can raise fallen man, as seeing eyes are the one only thing that can take away blindness from the man?

[App-3-6] If Adam had been able to undo himself all that he had done, if he could have gone back into that state from whence he was fallen, if he could have raised up again in himself that birth of the Holy Trinity, in which he was created, no savior had been wanted for him; but because he could not do anything of this, but must be that which he had made himself to be, therefore the wrath of nature, or the wrath of God, manifested in nature, abode upon him, and this wrath must of all necessity be appeased, atoned, and satisfied, that is, it must be kindled into light and love, before he could again find, and enjoy the God of nature, as a God of light and love.

[App-3-7] Could Adam himself have done all that which I have just now mentioned, then his own actions had atoned and satisfied the divine wrath, and had reconciled him to God: for nothing lost him the love of God, but that which separated him from God; and nothing did, or ever can separate him from God, but the loss of that inner triune life, in which alone the Holy Trinity of divine love can dwell. If therefore Adam could have raised again in himself that triune life, then his sin, and the wrath of God upon him, had been only transitory; but because he did that, which according to all the possibilities of nature, was unalterable; therefore he became a prisoner of an eternal wrath, and heir of an everlasting, painful life, till the love of God, who is greater than nature, should do that for him and in him, which he could by no powers of nature do for himself, nor the highest of creatures do for him.

[App-3-8] 3. And here we see in the plainest light, that there was no anger in God himself towards the fallen creature, because it was purely and solely the infinite love of God towards him, that did, and alone could raise him out of his fallen state: all scripture, as well as nature, obliges us to think thus of God. Thus it is the whole tenor of scripture, that "God so loved the world, that he sent his only-begotten Son into it, that the world, through him, might be saved": is not this saying more than if it had been said, that there was no anger in God himself towards fallen man? Is he not expressly declared to be infinitely flowing forth in love towards him? Could God be more infinite in love, or more infinitely distant from all possibility of anger towards man, when he first created him, than when he thus redeemed him? God out of pure and free love gave his Son to be the life of the world, first, as an inspoken and ingrafted Word of life, as the bruiser of the serpent given to all mankind in their father Adam. This Word of life, and bruiser of the serpent, was the extinguisher of that wrath of God that lay upon fallen man. Now, will the scriptures, which tell us that the love of God sent his Son into the world, to redeem man from that hellish wrath that had seized him, allow us to say, that it was to extinguish a wrath that was got into God himself, or that the bruiser of the serpent was to bruise, suppress, or remove something that sin had raised in the Holy Trinity itself? No surely, but to bruise, alter, and overcome an evil in nature and the creature, that was become man's separation from the enjoyment of the God of love, whose love still existed in its own state, and still followed

him, and gave his only Son to make him capable of it. Do not the holy scriptures continually teach us, that the holy Jesus became incarnate to destroy the works of the devil, to overcome death and hell that had taken man captive? And is not this sufficiently telling us, what that wrath was, and where it existed, which must be atoned, satisfied, and extinguished, before man could again be alive unto God, or reconciled unto him, so as to have the triune life of light and love in him? It was a wrath of death, a wrath of hell, a wrath of sin, and which only the precious, powerful blood of Christ could change into a life of joy and love: and when this wrath of death and hell are removed from human nature, there neither is, nor can be any other wrath of God abiding on it. Are not the devils and all lost souls justly said to be under the eternal wrath of God, and yet no wrath but that which exists in hell, and in their own hellish nature.

[App-3-9] 4. They therefore, who suppose the wrath and anger of God upon fallen man, to be a state of mind in God himself, to be a political kind of just indignation, a point of honorable resentment, which the sovereign Deity, as governor of the world, ought not to recede from, but must have a sufficient satisfaction done to his offended authority, before he can, consistently with his sovereign honor, receive the sinner into his favor, hold the doctrine of the necessity of Christ's atoning life and death in a mistaken sense. That many good souls may hold his doctrine in this simplicity of belief, without any more hurt to themselves, than others have held the reality of Christ's flesh and blood in the sacrament under the notion of the transubstantiation of the bread and wine, I make no manner of doubt: but when books are written to impose and require this belief of others, as the only saving faith in the life and death of Christ, it is then an error that ceases to be innocent: for neither reason nor scripture will allow us to bring wrath into God himself, as a temper of his mind, who is only infinite, unalterable, overflowing love, as unchangeable in love, as he is in power and goodness. The wrath that was awakened at the fall of man, that then seized upon him, as its captive, was only a plague, or evil, or curse that sin had brought forth in nature and creature: it was only the beginning of hell: it was such a wrath as God himself pitied man's lying under it; it was such a wrath as God himself furnished man with a power of overcoming and extinguishing, and therefore it was not a wrath that was according to the mind, will, and liking, or wisdom of God; and therefore it was not a wrath that was in God himself, or which was exercised by his sovereign wisdom over his disobedient creatures: it was not such a wrath, as when sovereign princes are angry at offenders, and will not cease from their resentment, until some political satisfaction, or valuable amends be made to their slighted authority. No, no; it was such a wrath as God himself hated, as he hates sin and hell, a wrath that the God of all nature and creature so willed to be removed and extinguished, that seeing nothing less could do it, he sent his only begotten Son into the world, that all mankind might be saved and delivered from it. For seeing the wrath that was awakened and brought forth by the fall, and which wanted to be appeased, atoned, and quenched, was the wrath of eternal death, and eternal hell, that had taken man captive; therefore God spared not the precious, powerful, efficacious blood of the holy Jesus, because that alone could extinguish this eternal wrath of death and hell, and re-kindle heaven and eternal life again in the soul. And thus all that the scriptures speak of the necessity and powerful atonement of the life and death of Christ, all that they say of the infinite love of God towards fallen man, and all that they say of the eternal wrath and vengeance to which man was become a prey, have the most solid foundation, and are all of them proved to be consistent, harmonious truths of the greatest certainty, according to the plain letter of scripture.

[App-3-10] 5. It is the foundation of the Law and the gospel, that without shedding of blood, there is no remission of sins; and that the precious blood of Christ could alone do this, could alone reconcile us to God, and deliver us from the wrath to come. How, and why blood, and only the blood of Jesus Christ could do this, will appear as follows: Adam was created with a twofold respect, to be himself a glorious, living, eternal image of the holy, triune God, and to be a father of a new world of like beings, all descended from himself: when Adam fell, he lost both these conditions of his created state; the holy image of God was extinguished, his soul lost the Light and Spirit of heaven, and his body became earthly, bestial, corruptible flesh and blood, and he could only be a father of a posterity partly diabolical, and partly bestial.

[App-3-11] Now, if the first purpose of God was to stand, and to take effect; if Adam was still to be the father of a race that were to become sons of God, then there was an absolute necessity that all that Adam had done in and to himself, and his posterity, by the fall, should be undone again; the serpent and the beast, that is, the serpentine life, and the bestial life in human nature, must both of them be overcome, and driven out of it. This was the one only, possible salvation for Adam, and every individual of his posterity.

[App-3-12] Adam had killed that which was to have been immortal in him, he had raised that into a life which never should have been alive in him, and therefore that which was to be undone and altered both in himself and his posterity, was this, it was to part with a life that he had raised up into being, and to get another life, which he had quite extinguished.

[App-3-13] And here appears the true, infallible ground of all the sacrifice, and all the blood-shedding that is necessary to redeem and reconcile man to God. 'Tis because the earthly, fleshly, bestial, corruptible life under the elements of this world, is a life raised and brought into man by the fall, is not that life which God created, but is an impurity in the sight of God, and therefore cannot enter into the kingdom of heaven; 'tis a life, or body of sin, brought forth by sin, and the habitation of sin, and therefore it is a life that must be given up, its blood must be poured out, before man can be released from his sins: this is the one only ground of all the shedding of blood in religion. Had not a life foreign to the kingdom of God, and utterly incapable of it, been introduced by the fall, there had been no possible room for the death of any creature, or the pouring out any blood, as serviceable and instrumental to the raising fallen man.

[App-3-14] 6. But now, this bestial, animal life which is thus to be given up, and its blood poured out, is but the half, and lesser half of that which is required to deliver man from all that the fall has brought upon him. For the heavenly life, the birth of the Light and Holy Spirit of God which Adam had quite extinguished, was to be kindled or regenerated again; also his first, glorious, immortal body was to be regained, before he could become an inhabitant of the kingdom of heaven: but for all this Adam had no power. See here again the true and dreadful state of the fall, it was the fall into such a life, as must be slain and sacrificed before the fallen soul could come to God; and yet this death and sacrifice of the body, which was thus absolutely necessary, was the most dreadful thing that could happen to man, because his own death, come when it would, would only remove him from the light of this world into the eternal darkness, and hellish state of fallen angels: and here we find the true reason, why man's own death, though a sacrifice necessary to be made, had yet nothing of atonement or satisfaction in it; it was because it left the eternal wrath of nature, and the hell that was therein, unquenched and unextinguished in the soul, and therefore made no reconcilement to God, no restoration to the creature of its first state and life in God, but left the soul in its dark, wrathful separation from the kingdom of light and love.

[App-3-15] But here the amazing infinity of divine love appeared, such a mystery of love as will be the universal song of praise to all eternity. Here God, the second person in the Holy Trinity, took human nature upon him, became a suffering, dying man, that there might be found a man, whose sufferings, blood and death had power to extinguish the wrath and hell that sin had brought forth, and to be a fountain of the first heavenly life to the whole race of mankind.

[App-3-16] It was human nature that was fallen, that had lost its first heavenly life, and got a bestial, diabolical life in the stead of it. Now if this human nature was to be restored, there was but one possible way, it must go back to the state from whence it came, it must put off all that it had put on, it must regain all that it had lost: but the human nature that fell, could do nothing of this, and yet all this must be done in and by that human nature which is fallen, or it could never, to all eternity, come out of the state of its fall; for it could not possibly come out of the state of its fall, but by putting off all that, which the fall had brought upon it. And thus stood man, as to all the powers of nature and creature, in an utter impossibility of salvation, and had only a short life of this world betwixt him and hell.

[App-3-17] 7. But let us now change scene, and behold the wonders of a new creation, where all things are called out of the curse and death of sin, and created again to life in Christ Jesus; where all mankind are chosen and appointed to the recovery of their first glorious life, by a new birth from a second Adam, who, as an universal redeemer, takes the place of the first fallen father of mankind, and so gives life and immortality, and heaven to all that lost them in Adam.

[App-3-18] God, according to the riches of his love, raised man out of the loins of Adam, in whose mysterious person, the whole humanity, and the Word of God was personally united; that same Word which had been inspoken into Adam at his fall, as a secret bruiser of the serpent, and real beginning of his salvation; so that in this second Adam, God and man was one person. And in this union of the divine and human nature lies the foundation and possibility of our recovery. For thus the holy Jesus became qualified to be the second Adam, or universal regenerator of all that are born of Adam the first. For being himself that Deity, which as a spark or seed of life was given to Adam, thus all that were born of Adam had also a birth from him, and so stood under him, as their common father and regenerator of a heavenly life in them. And it was this first inspoken Word of life which was given to Adam, that makes all mankind to be the spiritual children of the second Adam, though he was not born into the world till so many years after the fall. For seeing the same Word that became their perfect redeemer in the fullness of time, was in them from the beginning, as a beginning of their redemption, therefore he stood related to all mankind as a fountain and deriver of an heavenly life into them, in the same universal manner as Adam was the fountain and deriver of a miserable mortality into them.

[App-3-19] And seeing also this great and glorious redeemer had in himself the whole humanity, both as it was before and after the fall, viz., in his inward man the perfection of the first Adam, and in his outward the weakness and mortality of the fallen nature; and seeing he had all this, as the undoer of all that Adam had done, as the overcomer of death, as the former and raiser of our heavenly life, therefore it was, that all his conquests over this world, sin, death, and hell, were not the conquests of a single person that terminated in himself, but had their real effect and efficacious merit through all human nature, because he was the appointed father and regenerator of the whole human nature, and as such, had that same relation to it all as Adam had: and therefore as Adam's fall, sin and death, did not, could not terminate in himself, because he was our appointed father, from whom we must have such a state and condition of life as he had; so the righteousness, death, resurrection and ascension of Christ into the kingdom of heaven did not terminate in himself, but became ours, because he is our appointed second Adam, from whom we are to derive such a state and condition of life as he had; and therefore all that are born again of him, are certainly born into his state of victory and triumph over the world, sin, death and hell.

[App-3-20] 8. Now here is opened to us the true reason of the whole process of our savior's incarnation, passion, death, resurrection and ascension into heaven: it was because fallen man was to go through all these stages as necessary parts of his return to God; and therefore, if man was to go out of his fallen state, there must be a son of this fallen man, who, as a head and fountain of the whole race, could do all this, could go back through all these gates, and so make it possible for all the individuals of human nature, as being born of him, to inherit his conquering nature, and follow him through all these passages to eternal life. And thus we see, in the strongest and clearest light, both why and how the holy Jesus is become our great redeemer.

[App-3-21] Had he failed in any of these things, had he not been all that he was, and did all that he did, he could not have made one full, perfect, sufficient atonement and satisfaction for the sins of the whole world, that is, he could not have been and done that, which in the nature of the thing was absolutely necessary, and fully sufficient to take the whole human race out of the bondage and captivity of their fallen state. Thus, had he not really had the divine nature in his person, he could not have begun to be our second Adam from the time of the fall, nor could we have stood related to him as children, that had received a new birth from him. Neither could he have made a beginning of a divine life in our fallen nature, but that he was that God who could make our nature begin again where it had failed in our first father. Without this divinity in his person, the perfection of his humanity would have been as helpless to us as the perfection of an angel. Again, had he not been man, and in human nature overcome sin and temptation, he could have been no savior of fallen man, because nothing that he had done had been done in and to the fallen nature. Adam might as well have derived sin into the angels by his fall, as Christ had derived righteousness into us by his life, if he had not stood both in our nature, and as the common father and regenerator of it; therefore his incarnation was necessary to deliver us from our sins, and accordingly the scripture saith, "he was manifest in the flesh to destroy the works of the devil."

Again, if Christ had not renounced this life, as heartily and thoroughly as Adam chose it, and declared absolutely for another kingdom in another world; if he had not sacrificed the life he took up in and from this world, he could not have been our redeemer, and therefore the scripture continually ascribes atonement, satisfaction, redemption, and remission of sins to his sufferings and death. Again, had not our Lord entered into that state of eternal death which fallen man was eternally to inherit; had he not broken from it as its conqueror, and rose again from the dead, he could not have delivered us from the effects of our sins, and therefore the apostle saith, "If Christ be not risen, ye are yet in your sins." But I must enlarge a little upon the nature and merits of our savior's last sufferings. It is plain from scripture that that death, which our blessed Lord died on the cross, was absolutely necessary for our salvation; that he, as our savior, was to taste death for every man--that as the captain of our salvation, he was to be made perfect through sufferings-- that there was no entrance for fallen man into paradise till Christ had overcome death and hell, or that first and second death which stood between us and it.

[App-3-22] Now the absolute necessity of our savior's doing and suffering all this, plainly appears, as soon as we consider him as the second Adam, who, as such, is to undo all the evil that the first Adam had done in human nature; and therefore must enter into every state that belonged to this fallen nature, restoring in every state that which was lost, quickening that which was extinguished, and overcoming in every state that by which man was overcome. And therefore as eternal death was as certainly brought forth in our souls, as temporal death in our bodies, as this death was a state that belonged to fallen man, therefore our Lord was obliged to taste this dreadful death, to enter into the realities of it, that he might carry our nature victoriously through it. And as fallen man was to have entered into this eternal death at his giving up the ghost in this world, so the second Adam, as reversing all that the first had done, was to stand in this second death upon the cross, and die from it into that paradise out of which Adam the first died into this world.

[App-3-23] Now when the time drew near that our blessed Lord was to enter upon his last great sufferings, viz., the realities of that second death through which he was to pass, then it was that all the anguishing terrors of a lost soul began to open themselves in him; then all that eternal death which Adam had brought into his soul, when it lost the Light and Spirit of heaven, began to be awakened, and stirring in the second Adam, who was come to stand in the last state of the fallen soul, to be encompassed with that eternal death and sensibility of hell, which must have been the everlasting state of fallen man.

[App-3-24] The beginning of our Lord's entrance into the terrible jaws of this second death, may be justly dated from those affecting words, "My soul is exceeding sorrowful, even unto death, tarry ye here with me and watch." See here the Lord of life reduced to such distress as to beg the prayers, watching, and assistance of his poor disciples! A plain proof that it was not the sufferings of this world, but a state of dreadful dereliction that was coming upon him. O holy redeemer, that I knew how to describe the anguishing terrors of thy soul, when thou wast entering into eternal death, that no other son of man might fall into it.

[App-3-25] The progress of these terrors are plainly shown us in our Lord's agony in the garden, when the reality of this eternal death so broke in upon him, so awakened and stirred itself in him, as to force great drops of blood to sweat from his body. This was that bitter cup which made him withdraw himself, prostrate himself, and thrice repeat an earnest prayer, that if it were possible, it might pass from him, but at the same time heartily prayed to drink it according to the divine will.

[App-3-26] This was that cup he was drinking from the sixth to the ninth hour on the cross, nailed to the terrors of a twofold death, when he cried out, "My God, my God, why hast thou forsaken me?"

[App-3-27] We are not to suppose that our Lord's agony was the terrors of a person that was going to be murdered, or the fears of that death which men could inflict upon him; for he had told his disciples, not to fear them that could only kill the body, and therefore we may be sure he had no such fears himself. No, his agony was his entrance into the last, eternal terrors of the lost soul, into the real horrors of that dreadful, eternal death, which man unredeemed must have died into when he left this world. We are therefore not to consider our Lord's death upon the cross, as only the death of that mortal body which was nailed to it, but we are to look upon him with wounded hearts, as fixed and fastened in the state of that twofold death, which was due to the fallen nature, out of which he could not come till he could say, "It is finished; Father, into thy hands I commend my spirit."

[App-3-28] In that instant he gave up the ghost of this earthly life; and as a proof of his having overcome all the bars and chains of death and hell, he rent the rocks, opened the graves, and brought the dead to life, and triumphantly entered into that long shut up paradise, out of which Adam died, and in which he promised the thief, he should that day be with him.

[App-3-29] When therefore thou beholdest the crucifix, which finely represents to thy senses the savior of the world hanging on the cross, let not thy thoughts stay on any sufferings, or death, that the malice of men can cause; for he hung there in greater distress than any human power can inflict, forsaken of God, feeling, bearing, and overcoming the pains and darkness of that eternal death which the fallen soul of Adam had brought into it. For as Adam by his fall, or death in paradise, had nothing left in his soul, but the nature, properties and life of hell, all which must have awakened in him in their full strength, as soon as he had lost the flesh, and blood, and light of this world, as this eternal death was a state that belonged to man by the fall, so there was an absolute necessity that the savior of man should enter into all these awakened realities of the last eternal death, and come victoriously out of them, or man had never been redeemed from them. For the fallen nature could no way possibly be saved, but by its own coming victoriously out of every part of its fallen state; and therefore all this was to be done by that son of man, from whom we had a power of deriving into us his victorious nature.

[App-3-30] Lastly, if our blessed Lord was not ascended into heaven, and set on the right hand of God, he could not deliver us from our sins; and therefore the scripture ascribes to him, as ascended, a perpetual priesthood in heaven: "If any man sin," saith St. John, "we have an advocate with the Father, Jesus Christ the righteous, and he is the propitiation for our sins."

[App-3-31] All these things therefore are so many equally essential parts of our savior's character, and he is the one atonement, the full satisfaction for sin, the savior and deliverer from the bondage, power, and effects of sin. And to ascribe our deliverance from sin, or the remission of our sins more to the life and actions, than to the death of Christ, or to his death more than to his resurrection and ascension, is directly contrary to the plain letter and tenor of the scripture, which speaks of all these things as jointly qualifying our Lord to be the all- sufficient redeemer of mankind; and when speaking separately of any of them, ascribes the same power, efficacy, and redeeming virtue to one as to the other.

[App-3-32] And all this is very plain from the nature of the thing; for since all these things are necessary parts or stages of our return to God, every one of them must have the same necessary share in delivering us from our sinful state; and therefore what our savior did, as living, dying, rising from the dead, and ascending into heaven, are things that he did as equally necessary, and equally efficacious to our full deliverance from all the power, effects, and consequences of our sins.

[App-3-33] And here we may see, in the plainest light, how Christ is said to bear our iniquities, to be made sin for us, and how his sufferings have delivered us from the guilt and sufferings due to our sins, and how we are saved by him. It is not by an arbitrary, discretionary pleasure of God, accepting the sufferings of an innocent person, as a sufficient amends or satisfaction for the sins of criminals. This is by no means the true ground of this matter. In this view we neither think rightly of our savior, nor rightly of God's receiving us to salvation through him. God is reconciled to us through Jesus Christ in no other sense than as we are new born, new created in Christ Jesus. This is the only merit we have from him. Jesus Christ was made sin for us, he bore our iniquities, he saved us, not by giving the merit of his innocent unjust sufferings as a full payment for our demerits, but he saved us because he made himself one of us, became a member of our nature, and such a member of our nature, as had power to heal, remove, and overcome all the evils that were brought into our nature by the fall. He bore our iniquities and saved us, because he stood in our nature as our common father, as one that had the same relation to all mankind as Adam had, and from whom we can derive all the conquering power of his nature, and so are enabled to come out of our guilt and iniquities by having his nature derived into us. This is the whole of what is meant by having our guilty condition transferred upon him, and his merit transferred upon us: our guilt is transferred upon him in no

other sense than as he took upon him the state and condition of our fallen nature, to bear all its troubles, undergo all its sufferings, till he had healed and overcome all the effects of sin. His merit or righteousness is imputed or derived into us in no other sense, than as we receive from him a birth, a nature, a power to become the sons of God. Hence it appears, what vain disputes the world has had upon this subject, and how this edifying, glorious part of religion has been perplexed and lost in the fictions and difficulties of scholastic learning. Some people have much puzzled themselves and others with this question, how it is consistent with the goodness and equity of God to permit, or accept the sufferings of an innocent person as a satisfaction for the guilt and punishment of criminal offenders? But this question can only be put by those, who have not yet known the most fundamental doctrine of the gospel salvation; for according to the gospel, the question should proceed thus, How it is consistent with the goodness and equity of God, to raise such an innocent, mysterious person out of the loins of fallen man, as was able to remove all the evil and disorder that was brought into the fallen nature? This is the only question that is according to the true ground of our redemption, and at once disperses all those difficulties which are the mere products of human invention. The short of the matter is this:

[App-3-34] Man considered as created, or fallen, or redeemed, is that which he is, because of his state in nature; he can have no goodness in him when created, but because he is brought into such a participation of a goodness that there is in nature; he can have no evil in him when fallen, but because he is fallen from his good state in nature; he can no way be redeemed, but by being brought into his first state of perfection in nature; and therefore, this is an eternal, immutable truth, that he can be redeemed by the God of nature, only according to the possibilities of nature: and here lies the true ground, the whole reason of all that our savior was, and did, and suffered on our account: it was because in and through all nature there could be no other relief found for us: it was because nothing less than such a process of such a mysterious person could have power to undo all the evils that were done in and to the human nature; and therefore it is not only consistent with the goodness and equity of God to bring such a mysterious person into the world, but is the most infinite instance of his most infinite love to all mankind, that can possibly be conceived and adored by us. To proceed:

[App-3-35] 9. By the fall of our first father we have lost our first, glorious bodies, that eternal, celestial flesh and blood which had as truly the nature of paradise and heaven in it, as our present bodies have the nature, mortality and corruption of this world in them: if therefore we are to be redeemed, there is an absolute necessity that our souls be clothed again with this first paradisaical, or heavenly flesh and blood, or we can never enter into the kingdom of God. Now, this is the reason, why the scriptures speak so particularly, so frequently, and so emphatically of the powerful blood of Christ, of the great benefit it is to us, of its redeeming, quickening, life-giving virtue; it is because our first life, or heavenly flesh and blood is born again in us, or derived again into us from this blood of Christ.

[App-3-36] Our blessed Lord, who died for us, had not only that outward flesh and blood, which he received from the virgin Mary, and which died upon the cross, but he had also an holy humanity of heavenly flesh and blood veiled under it, which was appointed by God to quicken, generate, and bring forth from itself, such an holy offspring of immortal flesh and blood, as Adam the first should have brought forth before his fall.

[App-3-37] If our Lord Christ had not had a heavenly humanity, consisting of such flesh and blood as is not of this world, he had not been so perfect as Adam was, nor could our birth from him, raise us to that perfection, which we had lost, nor could his blood be said to purchase, ransom, redeem, and restore us; because, as it is heavenly flesh and blood that we have lost, so we can only have it ransomed and restored to us, by that blood which is of the same heavenly and immortal nature with that which we have quite lost. Our common faith, therefore, obliges us to hold, that our Lord had the perfection of the first Adam's flesh and blood united with, and veiled under that fallen nature, which he took upon him from the blessed virgin Mary. Had he not taken our fallen nature upon him, nothing that he had done, could have been of any advantage to us, or brought any ransom or redemption to our fallen nature; and had he not taken our nature as it was before the fall, he could not have been our second Adam, or a restorer to us of that nature, which we should have had from Adam if he had not fallen.

[App-3-38] Now, what our common faith thus fully teaches, concerning a heavenly, as well as earthly humanity, which our Lord had, is also plainly signified to us by several clear texts of scripture; as where he saith of himself, "I am from above, ye are from beneath," again, "I am not of this world," and further, "No one ascends into heaven, but he that came down from heaven, even the Son of Man, who is in heaven": these and other texts of the like nature, which plainly speak of something in our blessed Lord, which can neither be understood of his divinity, nor of that flesh and blood which he received from the virgin Mary, has forced some scholastic divines to hold the pre-existence of our savior's soul, which is an opinion utterly inconsistent with our redemption; for it is as necessary that our Lord should have a soul as well as a body derived from Adam, in order to be the redeemer of Adam's offspring: but all these texts, which a learning, merely literal, has thus mistaken, do only prove this great, necessary, and edifying truth, that our blessed Lord had a heavenly humanity, which clothed itself with the flesh and blood of this world in the womb of the virgin; and from that heavenly humanity, or life-giving blood it is, that our first heavenly, immortal flesh and blood is generated and formed in us again; and therefore his blood is truly the atonement, the ransom, the redemption, the life of the world; because it brings forth, and generates from itself the paradisaical, immortal flesh and blood, as certainly, as really, as the blood of fallen Adam brings forth and generates from itself the sinful, vile, corruptible flesh and blood of this life.

[App-3-39] Would you further know, what blood this is, that has this atoning, life-giving quality in it? It is that blood which is to be received in the holy sacrament. Would you know, why it quickens, raises and restores the inward man that died in paradise? The answer is from

Christ himself, "He that eateth my flesh and drinketh my blood, dwelleth in me, and I in him, that is, he is born of my flesh and blood." Would you know, why the apostle saith, "that he hath purchased us by his blood," Acts xx.28. "That we have redemption through his blood," Ephes.i.7. Why he prays, "the God of peace--through the blood of the everlasting covenant, to make us perfect in every good work to do his will"; 'tis because the holy Jesus saith, "except we drink his blood, we have no life in us," and therefore the drinking his blood, is the same thing as receiving a life of heavenly flesh and blood from him: and all this is only saying, that our savior, the second Adam, must do that for us and in us, which the first Adam should have done; his blood must be that to us by way of descent, or birth from him, which the blood of our first father, if he had not fallen, would have been to us; and as this blood of an immortal life is lost by the fall, so he from whom we receive it again by a secondary way, is justly and truly said, to purchase, to redeem, and ransom us by his blood.

[App-3-40] Now, there is but one redeeming, sanctifying, life-giving blood of Christ, and it is that which gave and shed itself under the veil of that outward flesh and blood that was sacrificed upon the cross; it is that holy and heavenly flesh and blood which is to be received in the holy sacrament; it is that holy, immortal flesh and blood which Adam had before the fall, of which blood, if we had drank, that is, if we had been born of it, we had not wanted a savior, but had had such flesh and blood as could have entered into the kingdom of heaven; had we received this holy, immortal flesh and blood from Adam before his fall, it had been called our being born of his flesh and blood; but because we receive that same flesh and blood from Jesus Christ, our second Adam, by our faith, our hunger and desire of it; therefore it is justly called our eating and drinking his flesh and blood.

[App-3-41] And here we have another strong scripture proof, that our savior had heavenly flesh and blood veiled under that which he received from the virgin Mary. For does not the holy sacrament undeniably prove to us, that he had a heavenly flesh entirely different from that which was seen nailed to the cross, and which was to be a heavenly, substantial food to us; that he had a blood entirely different from that which was seen to run out of his mortal body, which blood we are to drink of, and live for ever?

[App-3-42] Now, that flesh and blood cannot enter into the kingdom of God, is a scripture truth; and yet it must be affirmed to be a truth according to the same scriptures, that flesh and blood can, and must enter into the kingdom of God, or else, neither Adam, nor any of his posterity could enter in thither; therefore, it is a scripture truth, that there is a flesh and blood that has the nature, the likeness, and qualities of heaven in it, that is as wholly different from the flesh and blood of this world, as heaven is different from the earth. For if the flesh and blood that we now have, cannot possibly enter into the kingdom of heaven, and yet we must be flesh and blood, for ever in heaven; then it follows, that there is a real flesh and blood that has nothing of this world in it, that neither arises from it, nor is nourished by it, but will subsist eternally, when this world is dissolved and gone. Now, if this flesh and blood is lost by the fall of our first father, and if the blood which we derive from him is the cause, the seat, and principle of our mortal, corruptible, impure life; if from the blood of this first father, all our unholiness, impurity and misery is derived into us, then we may clearly understand what is meant by our being

redeemed by the blood of Christ, and why the scriptures speak so much of his atoning, quickening, life-giving, cleansing, sanctifying blood; it is because it is to us the reverse of the blood of Adam, it is the cause, the seat, the principle of our holiness and purity of life; it is that from which we derive an immortal, holy flesh and blood in the same reality from this second Adam, as we inherit a corrupt, impure, and earthly flesh and blood from our first Adam: and therefore that which would have been done to us by our birth, if we had been born of the holy blood of Adam unfallen, that we are to understand to be done to us, in and by the holy blood of Christ. For the blood of Christ is that to us in the way of redemption, which the blood of our first father should have been to us in the order of creation; for the redemption has no other end, but to raise us from our fall, to do that for us, which we should have had by the condition of our creation, if our father had kept his state of glory and immortality; and this is a certain truth, that there would have been no eating the flesh, and drinking the blood of Christ in the Christian scheme of redemption, but that the flesh and blood which we should have had from Adam, must of all necessity be had, before we can enter into the kingdom of heaven.

[App-3-43] 10. Here therefore is plainly discovered to us, the true nature, necessity and benefit of the holy sacrament of the Lord's Supper; both why, and how, and for what end, we must of all necessity, eat the flesh, and drink the blood of Christ. No figurative meaning of the words is here to be sought for, we must eat Christ's flesh, and drink his blood in the same reality, as he took upon him the real flesh and blood of the blessed virgin: we can have no real relation to Christ, can be no true members of his mystical body, but by being real partakers of that same kind of flesh and blood, which was truly his, and was his, for this very end, that through him, the same might be brought forth in us: all this is strictly true of the holy sacrament, according to the plain letter of the expression; which sacrament was thus instituted, that the great service of the church might continually show us, that the whole of our redemption consisted in the receiving the birth, spirit, life and nature of Jesus Christ into us, in being born of him, and clothed with a heavenly flesh and blood from him, just as the whole of our fall consists in our being born of Adam's sinful nature and spirit, and in having a vile, corrupt and impure flesh and blood from him.

[App-3-44] But what flesh and blood are we to eat and drink? Not such as we have already, not such as any offspring of Adam hath, not such as can have its life and death by, and from the elements of this world; and therefore, not that outward, visible, mortal flesh and blood of Christ, which he took from the virgin Mary, and was seen on the cross, but a heavenly, immortal flesh and blood, which came down from heaven, which hath the nature, qualities, and life of heaven in it, according to which our Lord said of himself, that he was a "Son of Man come down from heaven," that "he was not of this world," that "he was from above," &c., that very flesh and blood which we should have received from Adam, if we had kept his first glorious and immortal nature. For as the flesh and blood which we lost by his fall, was the flesh and blood of eternal life, so it is in the holy sacrament, that we may eat, and live for ever: this is the adorable height and depth of this divine mystery, which brings heaven and immortality again into us, and gives us power to become sons of God. Woe be to those who come to it with the mouths of beasts, and the minds of serpents! who, with impenitent hearts, devoted to the lusts of the flesh, the lusts of the eyes, and the pride of life, for worldly ends, outward appearances, and secular conformity, boldly meddle with those mysteries that are only to be approached by those that are of a pure heart, and who worship God in spirit and truth. Justly may it be said of such, that they eat and drink damnation to themselves, not discerning, that is, not regarding, not reverencing, not humbly adoring the mysteries of the Lord's body.

[App-3-45] If you ask how the eating and drinking the body and blood of Christ, is the receiving that flesh and blood of eternal life, which we should have had from Adam himself, it is for this plain reason, because the same kind of flesh and blood is in Christ, that was in Adam, and is in Christ as it was in Adam, for this very end, that it might be derived into all his offspring: so that we come to the sacrament of the blessed body and blood of Christ, because he is our second Adam, from whom we must now receive that eternal, celestial flesh and blood which we should have had from our first father; and therefore it is, that the apostle saith, the "first Adam was made a living soul," that is, had a life in himself, which could have brought forth an eternal ever-living offspring; but having brought forth a dead race, the last Adam, as the restorer of the life that was lost, was made a quickening spirit, because quickening again that life which Adam as a living soul, should have brought forth.

[App-3-46] And thus we have the plain and full truth of the most mysterious part of this holy sacrament, delivered from the tedious strife of words, and that thickness of darkness which learned contenders on all sides have brought into it. The letter and spirit of scripture are here both preserved, and the mystery appears so amiable, so intelligible, and so beneficial, as must needs raise a true and earnest devotion in everyone that is capable of hungering and thirsting after eternal life. And this true and sound knowledge of the holy sacrament could never have been lost, if this scripture truth had not been overlooked; namely, that Christ is our second Adam, that he is to do that for us, which Adam should have done; that we are to have that life from him, as a quickening spirit, which we should have had from Adam as a living soul; and that our redemption is only doing a second time, or in a second way, that which should have been done by the first order of our creation: this plain doctrine attended to, would sufficiently show us, that the flesh and blood of eternal life, which we are to receive from Christ, must be that flesh and blood of eternal life which we lost in Adam. Now, if we had received this immortal flesh and blood by our descent from Adam, we must in the strictness of the expression have been said to partake of the flesh and blood of Adam; so seeing we now receive it from Christ, we must in the same strictness of expression, be said to be real partakers of the flesh and blood of Christ, because he hath the same heavenly flesh and blood which Adam had, and for the same end that Adam had it; namely, that it may come by and through him into us. And thus is this great sacrament, which is a continual part of our Christian worship, a continual communication to us of all the benefits of our second Adam; for in and by the body and blood of Christ, to which the divine nature is united, we receive all that life, immortality, and redemption, which Christ, as living, suffering, dying, rising from the dead, and ascending into heaven, brought to human nature; so that this great mystery is that, in which all the blessings of our redemption and new life in Christ are centered. And they that hold a sacrament short of this reality of the true body and blood of Jesus Christ, cannot be said to hold that sacrament of eternal life, which was instituted by our blessed Lord and savior.

Printed in Great Britain
by Amazon